This catalogue accompanies the exhibition *tele-journeys*, organized by the MIT List Visual Arts Center, presented May 2–July 7, 2002.

Support for this exhibition has been provided by LEF Foundation, the Mondriaan Foundation, Amsterdam (supported by the Netherlands Culture Fund of the Dutch Ministries for Foreign Affairs and Education, Culture and Science), the Consulate General of The Netherlands in New York, The Netherland-America Foundation, the British Council, the Cultural Services of the French Embassy, the Council for the Arts at MIT, Cambridge SoundWorks, and Sound Seal.

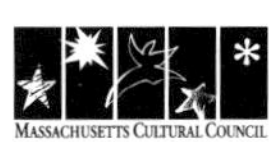 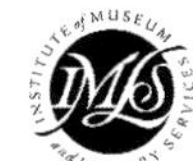

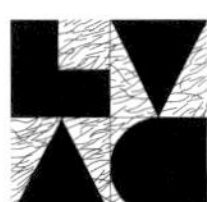

MIT List Visual Arts Center
Wiesner Building E15
20 Ames Street
Cambridge, MA 02139
(617) 253–4680
http://web.mit.edu/lvac

Catalogue designed by Linda Florio.
Printed and bound by Letter Perfect, Inc., Charlotte, NC.



ISBN: 0-938437-64-X

Cover: Runa Islam, *Tuin*, 1998, 2 DVDs projections,
2 CDs, 16 mm film.
Courtesy of Jay Jopling/White Cube, London.
Photo courtesy of Jay Jopling (London).

**CARLOS AMORALES**

**MARK BAIN**

**YAEL BARTANA**

**MICHAEL BLUM**

**SEBASTIAN DIAZ MORALES**

**NABILA IRSHAID**

**RUNA ISLAM**

**TOMOKO TAKE**

**FIONA TAN**

tele-journeys

Organized by Joan Jonas
Co-curator, Jane Farver

Introductions
by Joan Jonas and Jane Farver

Essay by Jens Hoffmann

MIT List Visual Arts Center

# journeys > by joan jonas

I first encountered most of the artists in *tele-journeys* while teaching at the Rijksakademie, an institution in Amsterdam where artists from all over the world convene, bringing with them their own cultural as well as personal and aesthetic references. In putting this show together, I did not begin with a particular agenda, but rather allowed the themes, which emerged from the artists I looked at, to start to define the direction of the exhibition. It interests me to find in the ideas of many young artists evidence of interpretations of different historical practices creating a fragmented vision of a contemporary reality. There is a sifting of '60's and '70's practices such as performance, conceptual art, and the multi-media approach, through deconstruction and the post-modern theorizing of the '80s and '90s, with added concerns such as popular culture, and ideas of the spectacle.

A notable aspect of the work of these artists is the more complex approach to sound and video as opposed to the single one-action gesture so familiar in art practices of the last decade. They layer elements of everyday rituals from popular culture with private histories, thus creating alternate personas, poetic documentary, and narratives that are affected by time and distance in moving from here to there. They make use of parallel disciplines, like anthropology and film-making, and specific historical works to transform our perceptions of familiar occurrences. Like the *bricoleur*, they transform and transmit information that would otherwise escape our attention, and use it to communicate different versions of the way the world looks and sounds.

As is, of course, the case when one artist is selecting the work of others, my own aesthetic concerns become apparent. I have always been interested in exploring and interacting with other cultures to develop my own performance rituals. At different times, I was inspired by the work of Artaud, Yeats, and Maya Deren, whose study of respectively, Eastern theatre, Mexican rituals, the Noh drama, and Haitian voodoo informed and enhanced the imagination of anyone who came in contact with their work. This process of borrowing and retelling is the way stories are finally made. What I find exciting about the present time is that distances have shrunk; and as it is often necessary for us to travel to work, these meetings, visits, and extended stays create a real dialogue of cultures. This show brings artists together who come from different places near and far. I wanted to present a group of works that draw from different sources—private and public—and that also utilize technology in particular ways, indicating a complexity of relationships. In doing so, other dialogues take place.

Finally, I would like to thank Jane Farver for inviting me to work with her on this exhibition. It was a thoroughly enjoyable collaboration.

# acknowledging... > by jane farver

*tele: Etymology: New Latin, from Greek tEle-, tEl-, from tEle far off -1 : distant : at a distance : over a distance 2 a : telegraph b : television c : telecommunication*[1]

Joan Jonas has chosen *tele-journeys* as the title for this exhibition; and the artists she has chosen to include in it, indeed, are voyagers. Educated in Europe[2]; they now live part or most of their lives there. They were born, however, in Argentina (Sebastian Diaz Morales), Bangladesh (Runa Islam), Germany (Nabila Irshaid), Indonesia (Fiona Tan), Israel (Yael Bartana and Michael Blum), Japan (Tomoko Take), Mexico (Carlos Amorales), and the United States (Mark Bain).

Over-used adjectives like peripatetic or nomadic could be used to describe these young artists, who live in multiple places, and travel around the world to make and present their work, relying on telecommunications and new technologies to do so. Are their works merely emblematic of the homogenizing effect of globalism? Does the fact that they nearly all work with the same medium indicate they have smartly adopted "Western" forms and concepts in their work to gain acceptance? Or, are there other possibilities?

Japan, Argentina, Germany, and the United States, each possess a four decade-long history of important conceptual and performance art; these were strong artistic movements that erupted and existed simultaneously. In Mexico and Israel, a similar history dates back to at least the 1970s; and artists in South Asia, Southeast Asia, and the Middle East have been actively involved with conceptual and performance art for a decade or longer. In many instances, artists in these areas adopted such practices to respond more effectively to destabilized, and often traumatic, situations in their regions that were brought on by larger political, economic, and social conditions of the time.

Throughout these particular postwar art histories, certain individuals have emerged who have practiced their art in more than one country, or on more than one continent. Their work bridged several (art)worlds, and defied easy categorization. Often unrecognized except by the prescient few in the early years of their practice, over time, their legacies have been claimed by other artists and art historians and marketplaces worldwide. Working between cultures, they created new artistic languages—or at least coined new words and phrases—to articulate their artistic responses to the ever-present problem of reconciling the global with the local. The works of artists such as Alberto Greco, Yoko Ono, Tehching Hsieh, Nam June Paik, David Medalla, David Llamelas, Yayoi Kusama, Luis Camnitzer, Billy Apple, and many others of the 1960s and '70s have come to symbolize this particularly fertile, fluid point in the history of art. Other artists since have carried on this tradition, as do those in this exhibition.

Electronic media and other new technologies have provided simultaneous instant access to information and images since the 1960s. For multiple generations, ubiquitous television, film, and video images literally have shaped how we see the world. So, it is not surprising that so many young artists around the world have adopted media-based technologies, finding (like their predecessors from the 1960s and '70s) that video still offers possibilities for the presentation of narrative, process, and concepts (personal and political) that other mediums do not. Video also offers a level of control to the artist not afforded by other mediums, since, to quote John Ravenel, it "unfolds at the artist's discretion."[3]

Each of the artists in *tele-journeys* has made some sort of artistic journey in an attempt to gain an understanding of their place in a complex world. Through the making of their works, Tomoko Take (*Dutch Wife, Dutch Life*) and Fiona Tan (*May You Live in Interesting Times*) each discovered things they didn't know about themselves and their families. Take found a father and sisters she was unaware of, and gained an understanding of her personal life choices. Tan traveled back through her family's complicated history to a Chinese village, to find that her identity must remain fluid, not fixed. *Rain*, Tan's second piece in *tele-journeys*, is a beautiful image about Asia and the passing of time, that seems to indicate her acceptance of that notion and willingness to observe and appreciate the beauty of that continent.

Other artists are working with journeys of the mind. Nabila Irshaid's work, *Travel Agency*, demonstrates that she can never be more than a tourist in her Palestinian father's psychic landscape—a landscape that has ceased to exist except in his memory and imagination.

Runa Islam traveled back to 1973 to reconstruct and deconstruct a 360° scene from Fassbinder's film, *Martha*. Islam's *Tuin* (or *Garden*) gives a nod to India's Bollywood film industry and the countless movies that have been made there using the same technique, and also examines the power structures at work in the original film.

Michael Blum's real and psychic journeys take him to a resort that epitomizes consumer luxury. There, he tries to take in the nature of global capitalism by reading Karl Marx's *Das Kapital* nearly one and a half centuries after it was first published. Another look at global capitalism is Sebastian Diaz Morales' *15,000,000 Parachutes*, made in Jakarta, Indonesia, with the cooperation of Ruang Rupa, an artists' organization formed and run by a number of Jakarta-based artists. Filtering spectacular travelogue imagery through a surrealist sensibility, the films pays homage to the city's approximately 4 million unemployed who continue to flow into the city from rural areas, hoping for jobs, even as Nike, Reebok, Adidas, and other footwear companies move their factories to China and Vietnam.[4]

An ever-present problem for artists (particularly those engaged in performance work, and who use their bodies in their art) is to find a way to articulate issues pertinent to the self without making the self literally the subject of the work. Carlos Amorales began *Amorales vs. Amorales* (a five-year-long series of works based on *luche libre*, the wildly popular world of Mexican wrestling) because he was "looking for an intermediary form that would allow me to involve my private life in my work, but at the same time avoid showing my personal life in public.... So I reinvented myself as the image of masked wrestler."[5] Impresario-like, Amorales also has facilitated the travel of Mexican wrestlers, artists, and intellectuals to Europe to participate in wrestling matches, conversations, and conferences; and that of European and U.S. artists and intellectuals to participate in events in Mexico. Documented in the videos in *tele-journeys*— the most comprehensive showing of these works to date—these events explore not just the social conventions of the popular wrestling world, but the art and business worlds as well.

Yael Bartana's two works in this exhibition *Profile* and *Trembling Time* are eloquent glimpses into contemporary life in her Israeli homeland that demonstrate the pervasive state of combat readiness exacted by the state of its citizens, and question what she calls "the power of ceremony on society and the individual."[6]

MIT alumnus Mark Bain has traveled back Cambridge to create the contribution to *tele-journeys*. Bain's *Sniffer*, which intercepts wireless data transmissions occurring inside the Wiesner Building that houses the MIT Media Lab as well as the List Visual Arts Center, is a "sonification": an actual registering of the usually inaudible electronic "noise" emanating from this extremely "wired" edifice. *Sniffer* is an apt metaphor for this exhibition. The artists in *tele-journeys* must also sift through torrential rivers of data (current events, personal, political, and artistic histories, popular culture, and many other influences) to find their own voices.

We at the List Visual Arts Center are grateful for this opportunity to accompany these young artists on their various sojourns. We also particularly wish to express our deep gratitude to artist Joan Jonas, guest curator for *tele-journeys*. Ms. Jonas unfailingly exhibited that all-too-rare combination of intelligence, generosity, and curiosity; working with her has been an unmitigated pleasure. We also express our sincere thanks to the artists for sharing their work and their time to be with us for this exhibition. We thank both essayist Jens Hoffman and designer Linda Florio for their contributions to this catalogue.

This project would not have been possible without the support of Lyda Kuth and Louisa McCall and the LEF Foundation; Taco de Neef, of the Mondriaan Foundation, Amsterdam (supported by the Netherlands Culture Fund of the Dutch Ministries for Foreign Affairs and Education, Culture and Science); Jeanne Wikler, Robert Kloos, and Wampie van der Wal of the Consulate General of The Netherlands in New York; The Netherland-America Foundation; Terri Evans of the British Council; Antoine Vigne, Frédéric Martel, and April Julich and the Cultural Services of the French Embassy; the Council for the Arts at MIT; Tim Leaver at Cambridge SoundWorks; Rich Mulcahy of Sound Seal. Finally, I gratefully acknowledge the superb work of the List Center for Visual Arts staff members on this project, particularly David Freilach, Tim Lloyd, John Rexine, Hiroko Kikuchi, Bill Arning, and Barbra Pine, and the assistance of interns Zeina Assaf, Paul Parcellin, and Almitra Stanley.

1 *Merriam-Webster Unabridged English Dictionary* on-line.

2 All but one studied at the Rijksakademie van Beeldende Kunsten, an important artists' residency/postgraduate program in Amsterdam, The Netherlands, where Joan Jonas teaches in addition to being a professor in the Visual Arts Program at MIT.

3 John Ravenal, "Introduction," *Outer & Inner Space: Pipilotti Rist, Shirin Neshat, Jane & Louise Wilson, and the History of Video Art.* With contributions by Laura Cottinham, Eleanor Heartney, and Jonathon Knight Crary. (Richmond, VA, 2002): 1.

4 See Michael Shari, "Indonesia's Economic State of Emergency," *Business Week Online*, 11 February 2002.

5 Carlos Amorales in —*los Amorales*. With contributions by Patricia Ellis, Cuauhtemoc Medina, Philippe Vergne, Rein Wolfs, Carlos Amorales; Marco Rascon, Sebastian Lopez et al. (Amsterdam: Stichting Artimo, 2001): 14, 20.

6 From a statement by the artist, 2002.

**passing silhouettes** > by jens hoffmann

"When there is no wind; the spiders…"
*Radovan Ivsic*[1]

As much as post-colonial thought has been a part of postmodern thinking, so have diverse interdisciplinary concepts. Looking at the field of the visual arts in the 1990s and significant exhibitions from that decade, the two topics that were discussed most extensively were postcolonial theory and ideas around various notions of interdisciplinarity. Where do they encounter each other, and where do they cross? They seem so far apart in the first moment, yet almost like brother and sister when looked at a second time. At the end of Gilles Deleuze's and Félix Guattari's book, *What is Philosophy*[2], the two authors discuss politics in ways other than in terms of ideology and identity. They speak about micro-politics and nomadic movements, and look into numerous disciplines to create what they call [philosophical] concepts: "philosophy needs a non-philosophy that comprehends it, just as art needs non-art and science needs non-science." They open a door for a nomadic, (de)territorialized understanding of art by rejecting borders of disciplines and discourses, not cultures and geographies alone, similar to Picabia's famous demand: "One must be a nomad, pass through ideas as one passes through countries and cities."[3]

The exhibition *tele-journeys*, organized by renowned U.S. visual artist Joan Jonas and List Visual Art Center Director Jane Farver, brings together various issues related to the crossing of cultures, discourses, and different artistic fields by presenting the work of nine artists who are part of an interdisciplinary and globalized generation. Coming from places as disparate as Israel, Mexico, the USA, Germany, Bangladesh, Argentina, and Japan, a number of the artists have deliberately chosen to be dislocated from their own distinct cultural background in order to enter yet another clearly-shaped cultural context; others have grown up in-between cultures. They have settled into the cultural hybridity of Europe, but carried along the knowledge, experience, and traditions of their homes. In addition, they travel around the globe in a seemingly everyday manner, and are precisely those nomadic protagonists of an existence that produces— and in fact is—something that has frequently been referred to as the "Third Space." This is a cultural condition in which people are not unequally joined together anymore, but a situation of hybridity and transnational spheres taking place between the private and the public, between identity and politics.

*tele-journeys* includes a series of video installations and film or video works that are either projected onto screens or shown on TV monitors. The use of video and film has been characteristic of most of our recent experience with the unstable side of globalization; and it is, maybe as a consequence of that, also the means through which we will encounter most artists' concepts in this exhibition.

Originally from Mexico City, the artist Carlos Amorales has lived in Amsterdam since 1996, having remained there after finishing school in 1998. During the last five years, he has developed a series of works that deal with a particular phenomenon of Mexican culture, wrestling. Like wrestling from the United States that has gained popularity even in Europe, Asia, and Africa, Mexican wrestling is an essential part of popular culture in the region. Its history and traditions, however, are quite different. Instead of being purely a commercial undertaking of global proportions, Mexican wrestling is a phenomenon that is closely linked to issues within small communities throughout the country (at the same time as it is a marketable spectacle). The wrestlers defend the ethics and moral codes of a seemingly long-lost time. Subjects of identification for many young kids in

Mexico, they appear on TV to fight for the rights of the discriminated-against and the poor, attacking drug dealers, pimps, and other criminals, as well as dubious real-estate companies and even the local government. Amorales has made a variety of works on this topic. He has staged several real-life fights in museums and other art institutions, as well as in wrestling arenas in Mexico; studied the making of the wrestlers' costumes; conducted interviews with wrestlers of all ages; and worked with the very specific graphics on posters and leaflets that announce the wrestling matches. He has interviewed the mask-maker Ray Rosas and even invented a character called Amorales who appears regularly in his works. This character is at the center of video works and graphics that constitute his installation for *tele-journeys* which will include among other works, *Amorales Interim* (1997), *In Conversation with Ray Rosas* (1997), and the four-channel video installation, *Amorales vs. Amorales* (1999).

Unlike the other artists in the exhibition, U.S. artist Mark Bain does not work with screens or projected images. He insists on the audio-image instead of following the contentions between "screen" and "image," to use Paul Virilio's terms. For the exhibition at LVAC, Bain has conceived a device called *Sniffer* (2002) that intercepts wireless data transmissions at MIT's Media Lab near the gallery space. The signals it receives are converted into an audio output, creating a flow of noise similar to what we already experience in our highly technological contemporary life, but usually only on a subconscious level. Bain records the noise that is behind, or more precisely, within, many of the tools and gadgets used to make our planet an apparently smaller and smaller place. Radio, TV, cell phones, and countless other wireless data-sending devices all relate in one way or the other to the situation we are experiencing as globalization. Invisible, they are in fact the foundations of much of the communication and interaction on our planet.

Runa Islam has lived in England since her early childhood, and is part of the large Bangladeshi community in London. She uses various media including photography and video; and she is working within a tradition begun by a generation of contemporary European artists that emerged in the early 1990s who were appropriating issues of cinema and incorporating extracts of, and references to, classic films into their work. Islam's films are short and subtle, so short and subtle that one gets the impression of witnessing only a little moment, a small scene, a form of animated in-between of a scenario that never discloses itself entirely to the viewer. Remembering the movies of Jean-Luc Godard or Michelangelo Antonioni, we understand that there is hardly anything else than the in-between. Islam captures the aesthetics, subtlety, and active inactivity of her favorite directors, making us aware that film is nothing more than the idea of still images moving in front of our eyes. *Tuin* (1998), the film shown in this exhibition, is based on a particular scene in German filmmaker Rainer Werner Fassbinder's 1973 film, *Martha*, and the director's lifelong obsession with disclosing the tragedy behind seemingly everyday human relationships. As Islam states, the particular scene she recreated is an archetypal feature of Hollywood; and it could be the pure cliché of what a Western audience would expect from a Hollywood film as well: a 360° camera shot of a couple who meet briefly and take leave of each other. Islam dismantles this classic form of shooting an encounter of tangled characters seemingly spinning around each other by shooting the camera crew in the background as well. She states, "The 360° track becomes a very important motif.... I think the moment in the film when the man eclipses the woman is very important, not necessarily for feminist reasons, but for any person whose identity has been overshadowed by another's."[4]

While most works shown in *tele-journeys* are in different ways related to the artists' personal histories and backgrounds, or at least incorporate references to them, Tomoko Take's series of documentary videos *Dutch Wife/Dutch Life* (1998) is simply about her own family history. Take is on the search for her father, who left her and her mother to live with another woman. During the first part of the film, we see Take's mother telling stories about her life and her various jobs, and how she got pregnant by one of her clients while working in an amusement bar. Take investigates this story, and actually manages to find her anonymous father. She convinces her mother to meet him, and it is surprising how well everyone seems to get on with each other once they are together again. The second part of the film shows Take's newly established relationship with her father and his views on the relationship that he had with her mother. The title of the film is a reference to a rather peculiar connection between Japan and Holland: "Dutch wife" is the Japanese expression for sex-doll or prostitute. The origin of this term goes back to colonial times in Indonesia where the British, making fun of the Dutch, named a particular pillow the Dutch would carry around to sleep on, a pillow that would let them sleep cool in the humid climate of South-East Asia, "Dutch wife." Take also has made sex-dolls modeled after her own body with faces and costumes similar to hers that she has used in her installations and performances. The work tells a very personal story, something many people would probably not talk about in public even though we all know about the presumably dark sides that are a part of every family's history.

*Travel Agency* (2001) is a short film made by Nabila Irshaid, an artist of Palestinian and German descent currently living in Austria. The work, based on several short super-8 films shot by her father in the 1970s while on a journey through the Middle East, is an autobiographical attempt to understand and correct today's public image of her cultural heritage and origins, as well as the contemporary situation of the Palestinians. The artist stated that one of her aims was to show how diverse Palestinian culture actually is in contrast to the mostly negative image most people have. We see different scenes in the film: everyday situations in Jerusalem and Bethlehem and various shots of deserts and rivers. The film has been left in its original condition, and some faded scenes are barely identifiable. The artist's accompanying comments describe the scenes as if the Middle East were a quiet and peaceful area of the world; and the images suggest the same. Irshaid attempts to understand her father's nostalgia for his homeland in view of the current violent political situation, and asks if the degraded image of the film corresponds in any way to the possibly unrecoverable condition of former life in the Middle East.

Similarly, Yael Bartana's works aim to expose everyday situations behind the clichéd images of the current state in the Middle East. When I saw her video *Trembling Time* (2001) for the first time, I did not know I had witnessed a common scene that takes place on Soldiers' Memorial Day in Tel Aviv. At first, it looked like part of a science-fiction movie, the moment people discover a large UFO in the sky, and all stare in one direction. Filmed from an overpass onto a busy highway, *Trembling Time* shows the steady flow of cars on the road coming to a full stop, and people silently getting out of their cars to remember those who have been killed. The film is alienating, especially when one does not know exactly what one is watching. The artist overlaid the images with a sound similar to tanks or train brakes, and once the moment of grieving is over, all cars start to move again just like before. The artist questions a moment of collectivity as imposed by the state, a collectivity that is in fact so important for the country and the culture from which she comes. The second film Bartana presents, *Profile* (2000), mirrors a more familiar image we have of the Middle East. We see a group of young, female Israeli soldiers training to shoot machine guns. They load their weapons and fire at targets in the shape of enemy soldiers until they run out of ammunition. As in the artist's other film, her effective but distressing use of slow motion allows us to see the situation more precisely, and to recognize these young women's obvious fear.

*Wandering Marxwards*, Michael Blum's 1999 film, contrasts Karl Marx's well-known exploration of early capitalist systems, *Das Kapital*, with today's hyper-capitalistic globalized economy. Blum placed himself, 132 years after *Das Kapital* was originally published, in the bizarre scenery of a Rocky Mountain holiday resort. In the film, we see Blum exploring the vacation spot to which he has transplanted himself, taking part in different forms of companionless leisure activities: shopping, working out at the gym, relaxing in the Jacuzzi, having breakfast, or simply lying in the sun. What appears to be at first glance a family video documenting Blum's holiday in a ski resort, turns out be a quest for questions with no answers. The resort is deserted and almost completely abandoned, which comes as no surprise as Blum has shot this short film during the summer. The desolate, faceless scenery of the city contrasts with Marx's arguments and Blum's elaborations on them, creating a scenario that, even though occasionally amusing, discloses the pure horror of alienation in Western societies. It is a political work incorporating a bit of tongue-in-cheek humor. At the end of the film, Blum is asked by a female voice not to forget Leon Trotsky's writings and theories, and Blum moves on with his search, leaving *Das Kapital* behind next to the bubbling whirlpool.

*May You Live In Interesting Times* (1997), one of Fiona Tan's two contributions to this exhibition, seems like a distillation of the many issues examined in the various works of art shown in *tele-journeys*—the pursuit of identity. In the beginning of the documentary, which is mainly based on interviews with family members spread around the world and historic film footage, Tan asks two essential questions: "Who am I?" and "Where do I come from?" The film is an attempt to find answers to these questions. Tan, as the daughter of a Chinese father from Indonesia and an Australian mother of Scottish origin, has spent the last 15 years of her life in Europe while her parents and siblings live in Australia where Tan was born. The question that comes up, inevitability, is the problem of defining what identity actually is. What makes Tan's film unique is the conclusion that nationality and culture are not absolute criteria that determine one's identity, but rather an unstable assemblage of influences that remain in flux. The work creates a very personal bond between artist and audience that is of such intimacy that her film, in all its instability,

comes across almost as a form of universal truth of our global identity.

The startling economic collapse of Argentina at the end of 2001 is something that Sebastian Diaz Morales might not have experienced first-hand, as he has lived in Amsterdam in recent years. His short-film, *15,000,000 Parachutes* (2001), however, tells of an economic crisis from the other side of the earth in Indonesia. The title refers to the number of people living in Indonesia's capital Jakarta, which until the late 1990s was considered one of the most stable and economically fastest-growing cities in the emerging markets of Southeast Asia. Today, Indonesia is still among the rather stable economies of the region, but the boom and the prosperity of the 1990s have vanished. It is hard to actually place Diaz Morales' film geographically, as the city appears to be a blur of highways, monuments, and skyscrapers in a polluted metropolis. But there is also much beauty in the film, a beauty that comes to the viewer in the poetic images selected by the artist and through his use of the metaphor of the parachute as an object for survival.

After viewing this selection of works from this younger generation, it could appear that the concepts of multiculturalism of the 1980s and the postcolonial theories of the 1990s do not seem to matter that much anymore. Rather, they could be seen as a part of what American art historian Thomas McEvilly, recently called the "second generation of multiculturalism."[5] Indeed, there is a difference when looking at some of the significant exhibitions of the past that related to ideas of transculturality and multiculturalism.[6] This situation seems to have changed when many artists in today's exhibitions tackling these subjects are displaced from their original cultural backgrounds and fused with Western positions, as this exhibition also shows. But *tele-journeys*, and most of the works in the show, are not exercises in multiculturalism; they are, rather, very personal takes on today globalized society.

1 Translated from Radovan Ivsic, *Quand il n'y a pas de vent, les araignées* (Paris: Contre-Moule, 1986).

2 Gilles Deleuze with Félix Guattari, *What Is Philosophy?* trans. Hugh Tomlinson and Graham Burchell (New York: Columbia University Press, 1996), 218.

3 Francis Picabia in *The Dada Painters and Poets*, ed. Robert Motherwell (New York: Wittenborn Schultz, 1951), 206.

4 See Runa Islam and David Bussel in <hers> *Video as a Female Terrain*, ed. Stella Rollig (New York: Springer-Verlag Wien, 2000).

5 From "Aspect of Quality," a lecture given by Thomas McEvilly for *Under Construction*, a conference held 12-13 October 2001, at the Finnish Theatre Academy in Helsinki, and organized by the Nordic Institute for Contemporary Art (NIFCA), in collaboration with the Nordic Council of Ministers, the Finnish Ministry of Education, and Nordic Theatre and Dance (*TODIN*).

6 The one exhibition that supposedly started it, *Magiciens de la Terre* (1989), for example, involved art of more than one hundred Western and non-Western artists. However most of the artists from non-Western places (such as Zairian artist Cheri Samba) were still living in their home countries.

CARLOS AMORALES

MARK BAIN

YAEL BARTANA

MICHAEL BLUM

SEBASTIAN DIAZ MORALES

NABILA IRSHAID

RUNA ISLAM

TOMOKO TAKE

FIONA TAN

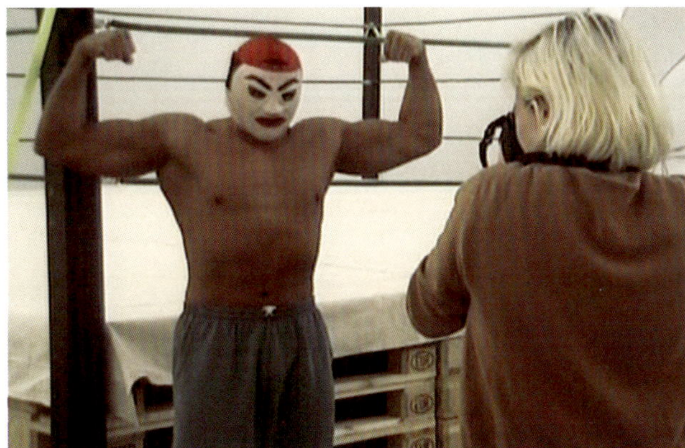
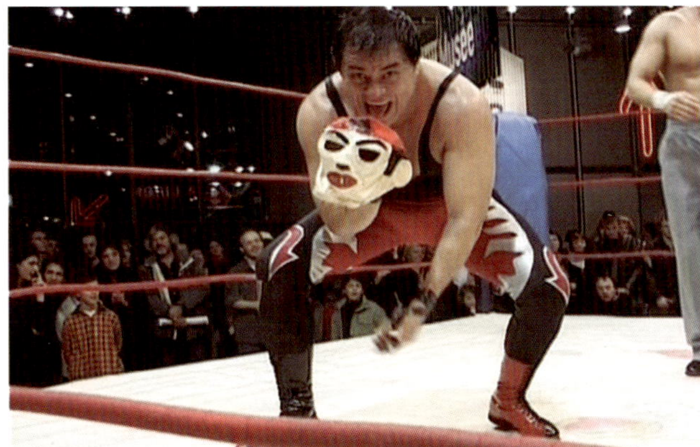
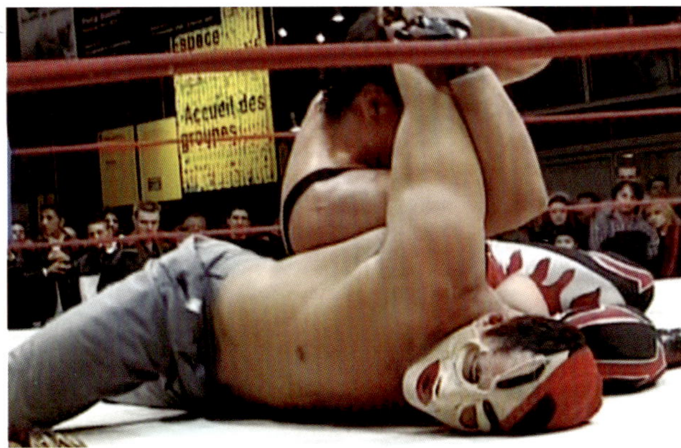
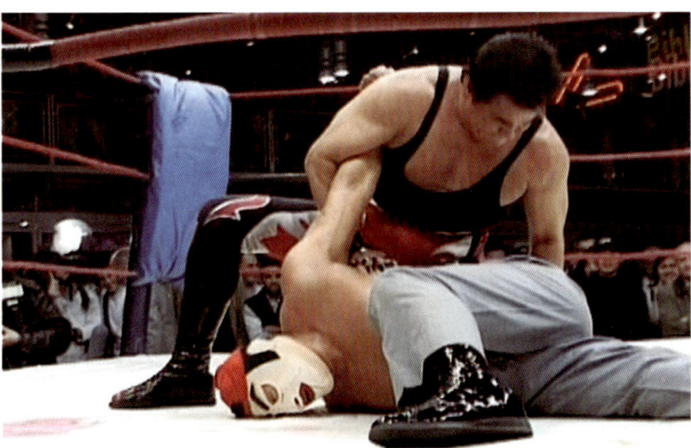

*Amorales vs. Amorales*, 1990–2001
DVDs (*El Olympico* and *Amorales*); monitors
Collection MGB, Migros Museum für
Gegenwartskunst, Zurich

"An intermediary form that allows involving one's private life in the artwork, at
the same time to avoid showing one's personal life in public."

Carlos Amorales in —*los Amorales*. With contributions by
Patricia Ellis, Cuauhtemoc Medina, Philippe Vergne, Rein Wolfs,
Carlos Amorales, Marco Rascon, Sebastian Lopez et al.
(Amsterdam, Stichting Artimo, 2001): 51.

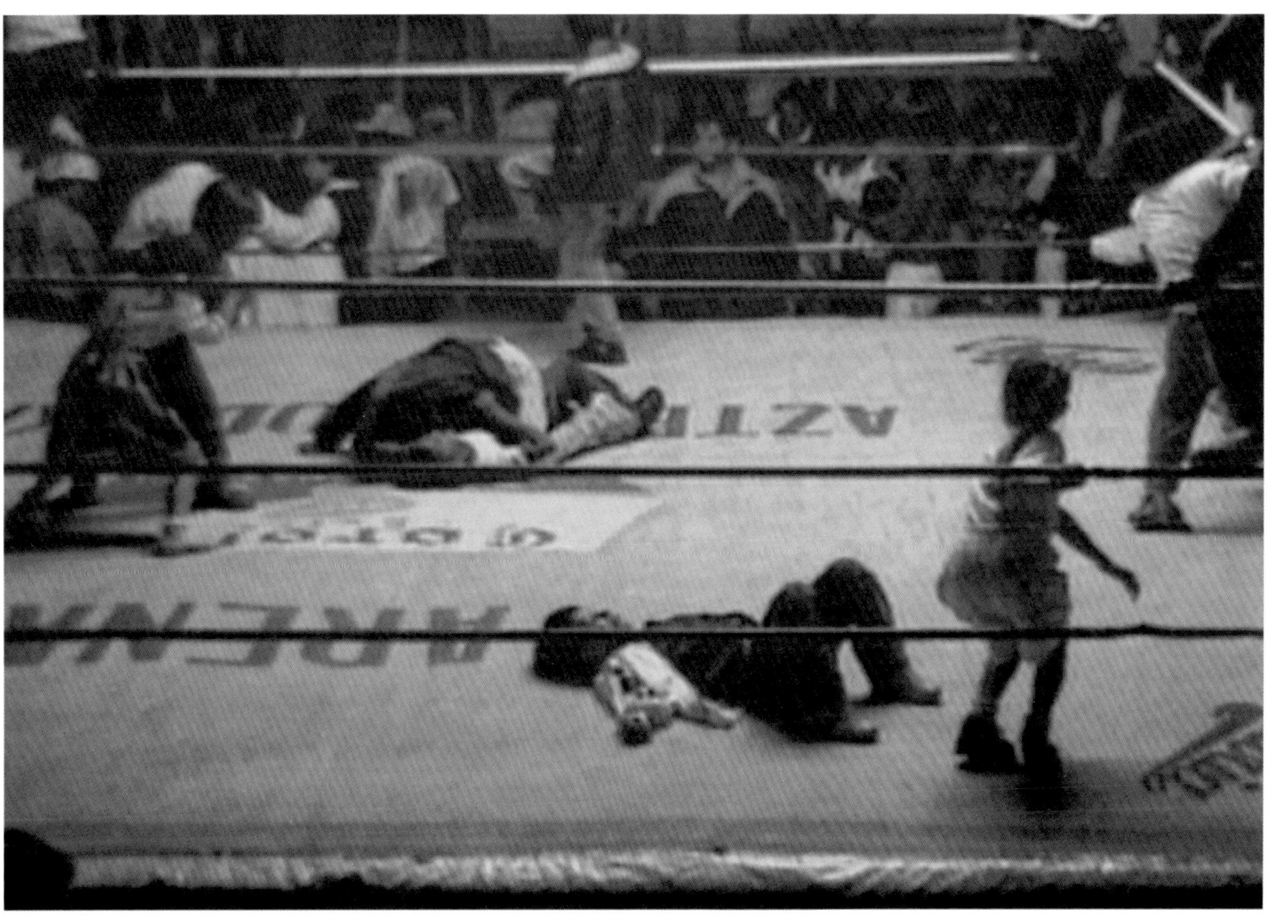

*Solitario* (Solitary), 1998
VHS videotape on monitor
Collection Walker Art Center, Minneapolis
T.B. Walker Acquisition Fund, 1999

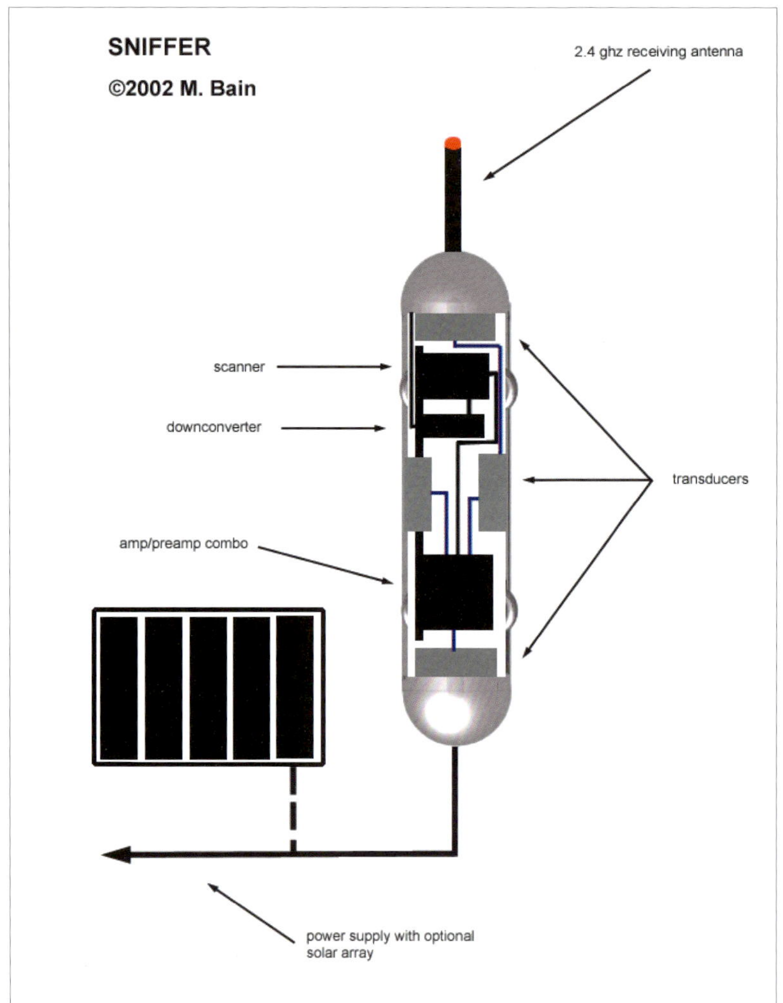


*Sniffer*, 2002
Steel, aluminum, electronic components
Courtesy of the artist

"The signal it collects is downconverted as a direct audio output of the exact sound of data, not a synthetic representation, but as a registration of the flow of noise that surrounds us constantly. It is a signal diviner, a transducer of 0s and 1s and speed."

From a statement by the artist, 2002.

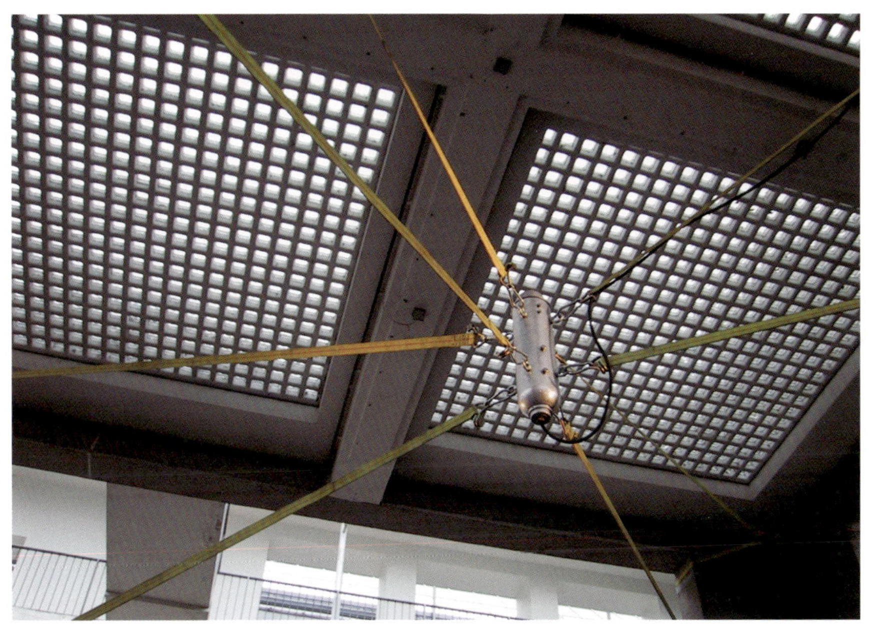

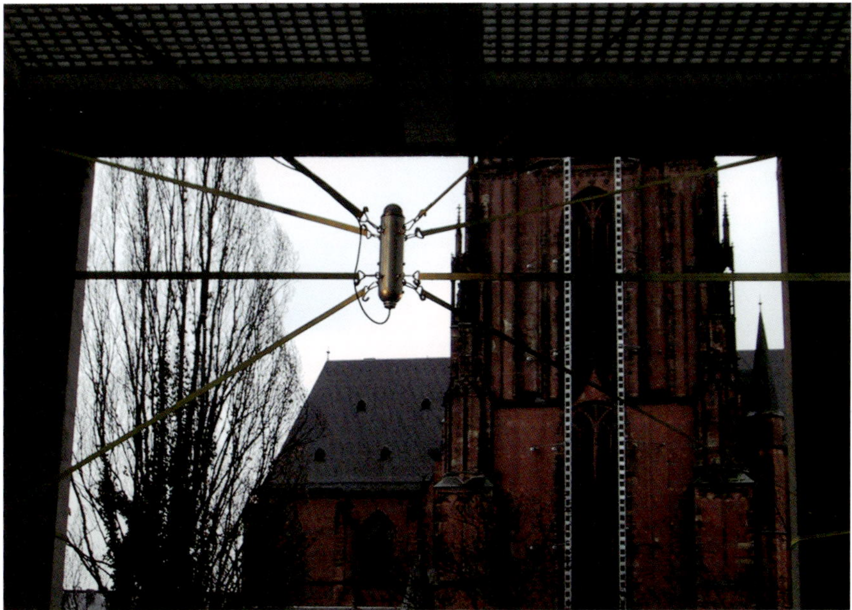

*The Pill*, 2002
Steel, mechanized oscillators, 150cm x 20cm
Schiren Kunsthalle, Frankfurt, Germany

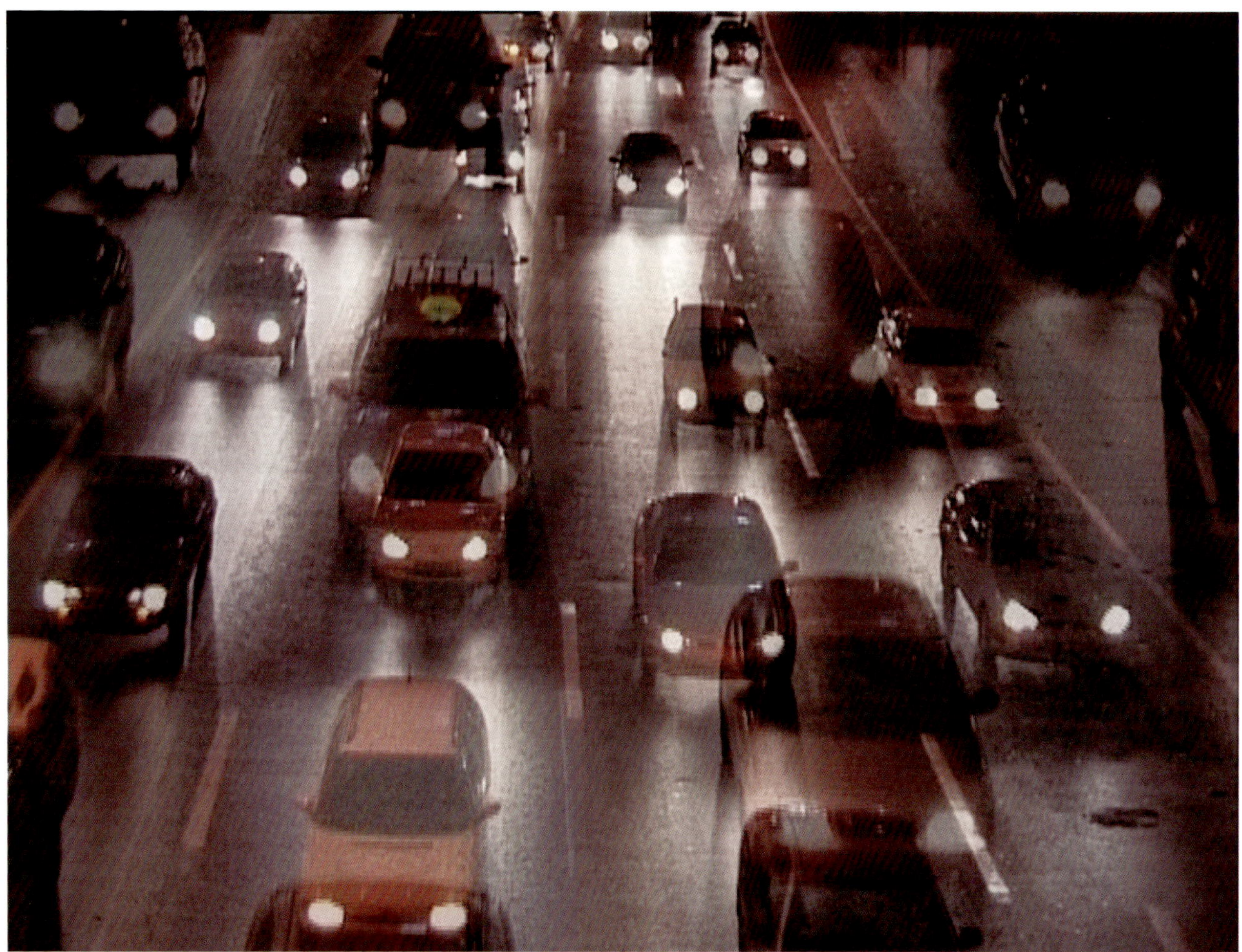

*Trembling Time*, 2001
DVD projection
Courtesy of the artist

"*Trembling Time* transforms the event into an object, and questions the power of ceremony on society and the individual."

From a statement by the artist, 2002.

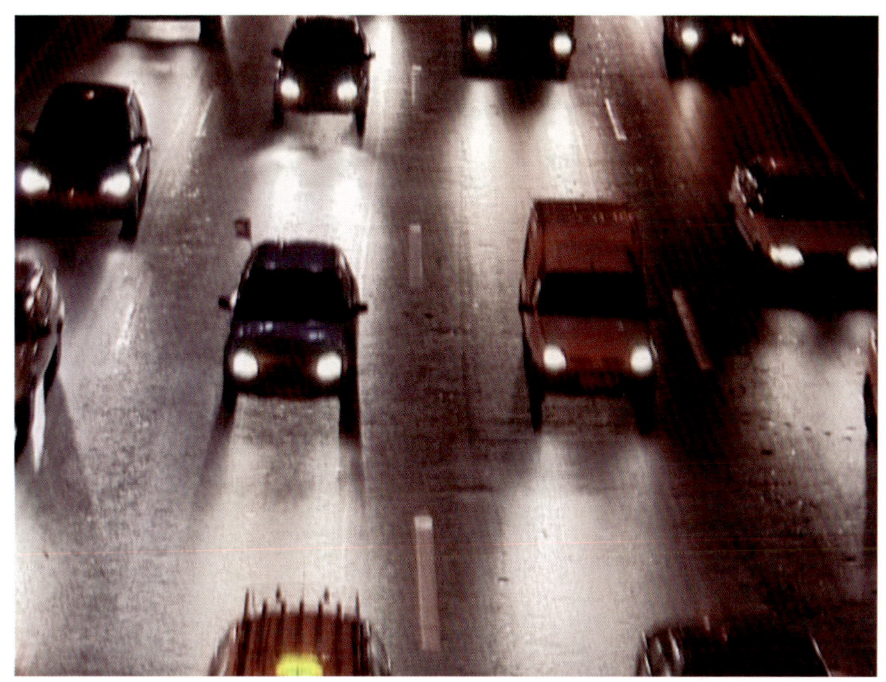

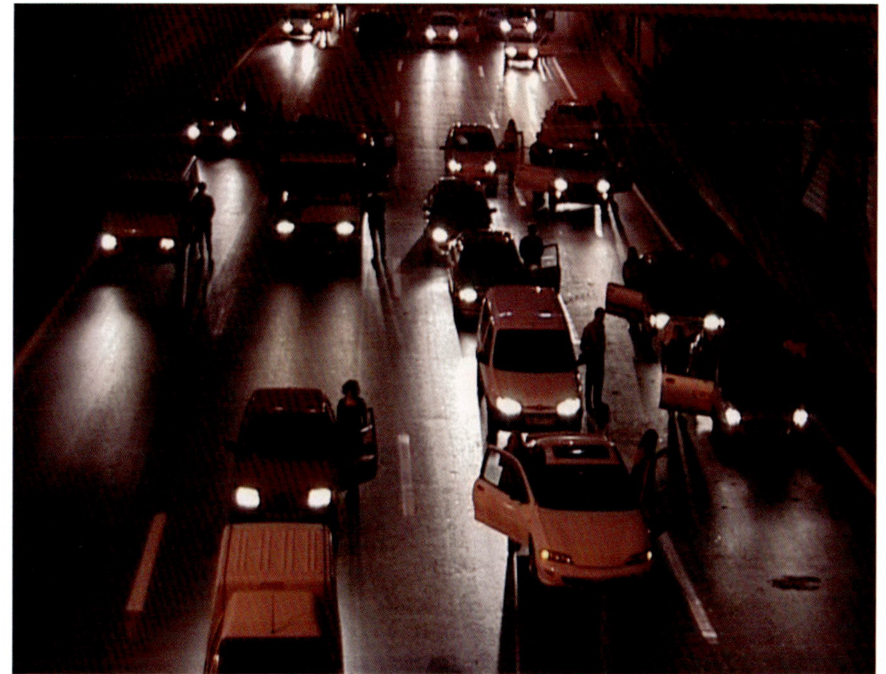

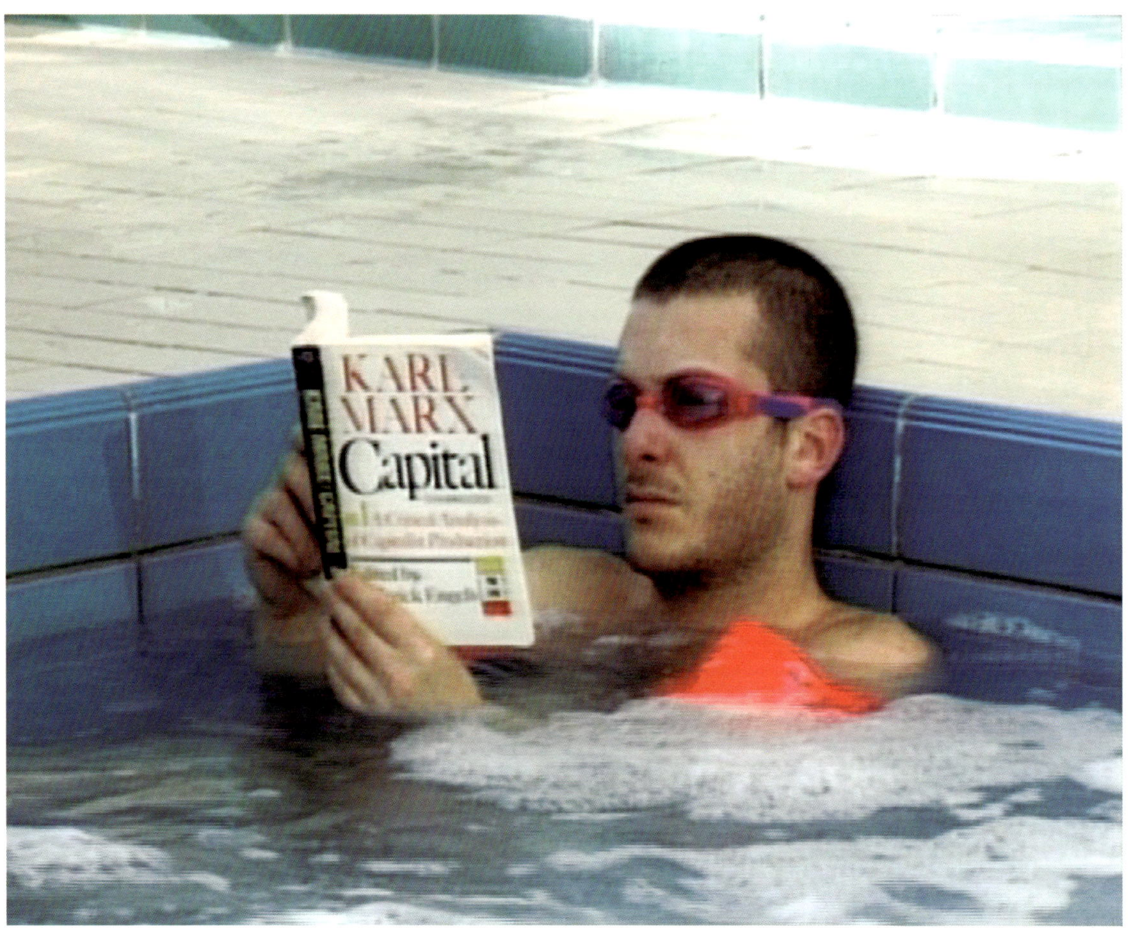

*Wandering Marxwards*, 1999
VHS videotape, monitor
Courtesy of the artist

"Filming Capital was too much for me, or I was too little for
filming Capital"

From a statement by the artist, 2002.

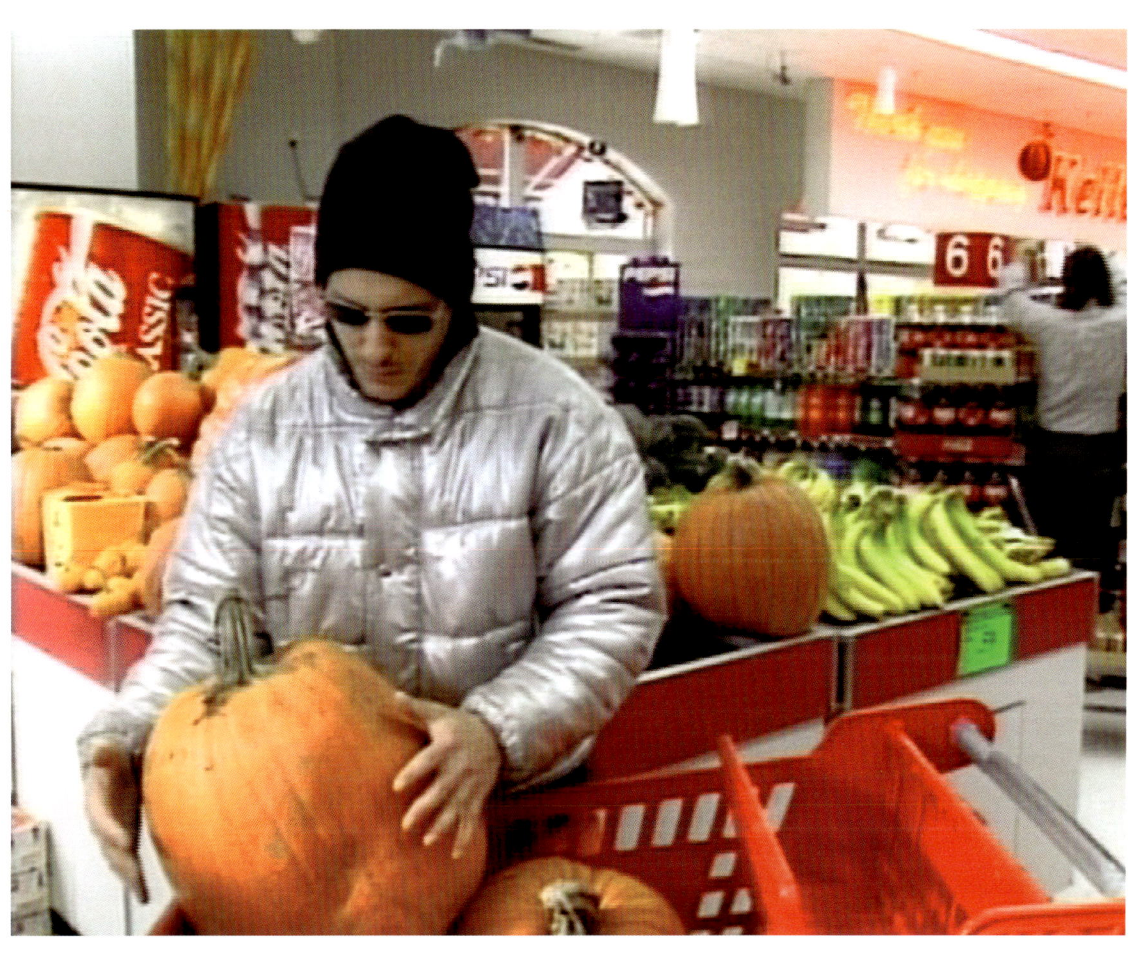

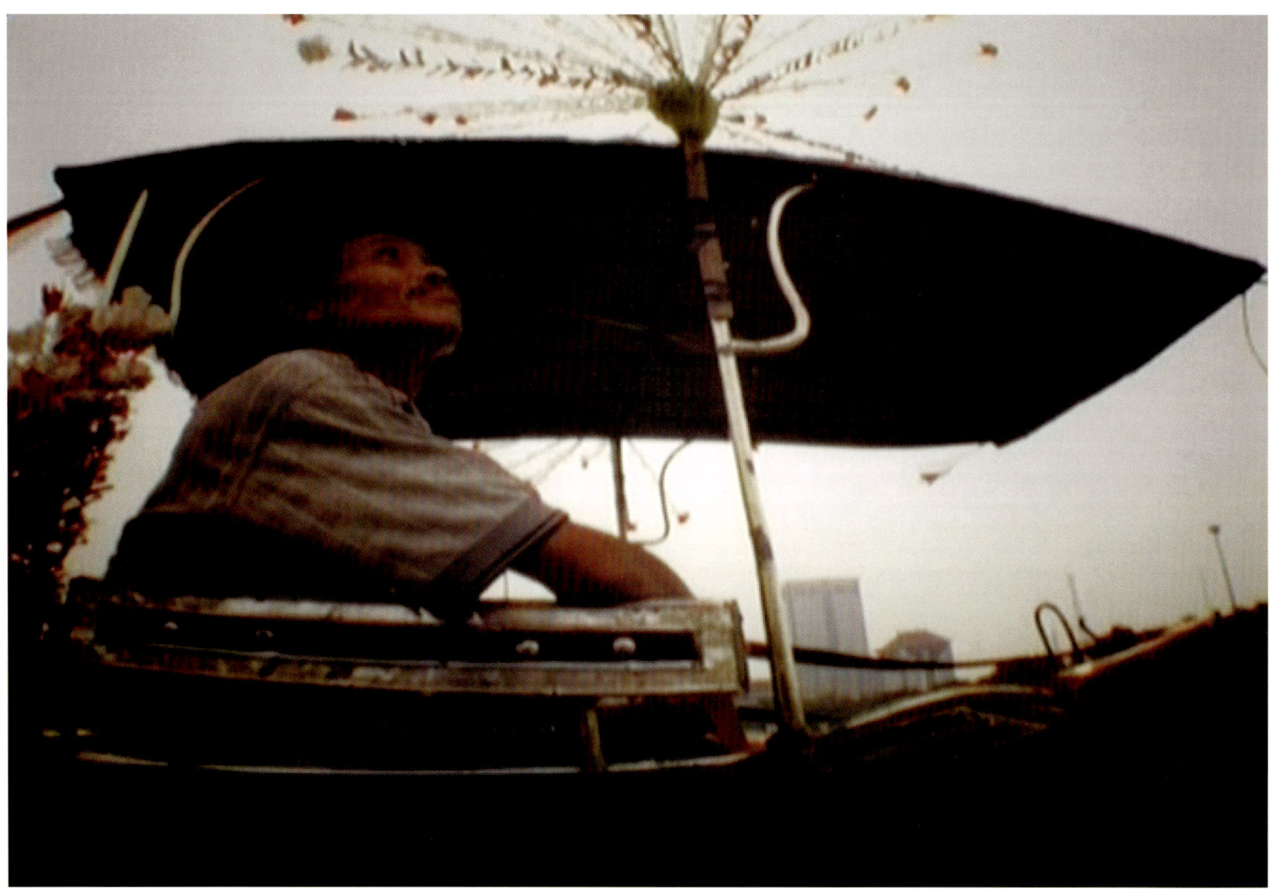

*15,000,000 Parachutes*, 2001
DVD projection
Courtesy of the artist

"First is an act, an extraordinary or unusual situation, or even a movie that makes the
author, that makes a character, and the viewer, to be able to perceive what surrounds
him or her in a different way. After that, thought of discovering the illusion takes
part. Illusion of getting somewhere, of doing, of finding more. Is the illusion then,
the second motor of things?"

From a statement by the artist, 2002.

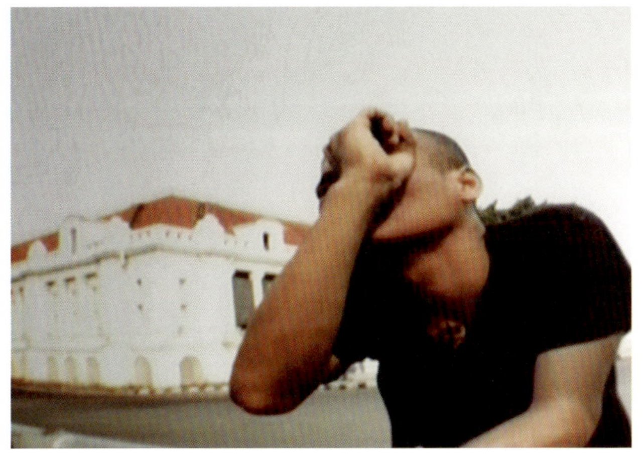

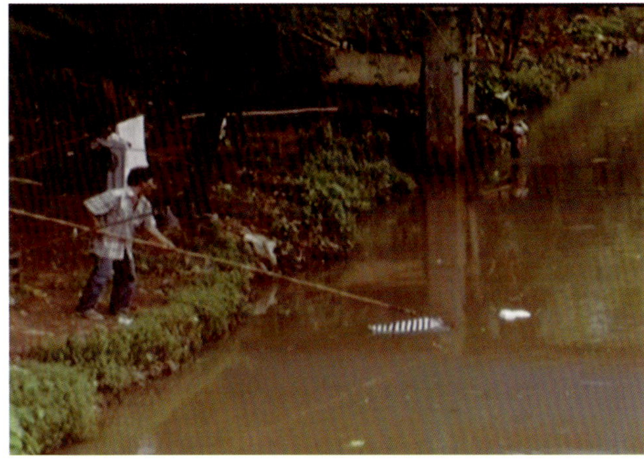

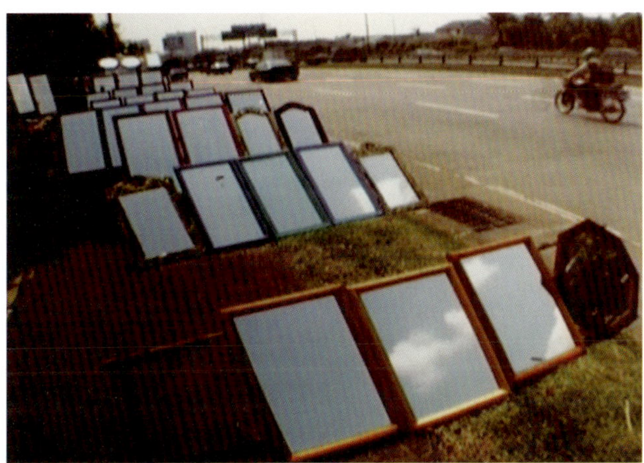

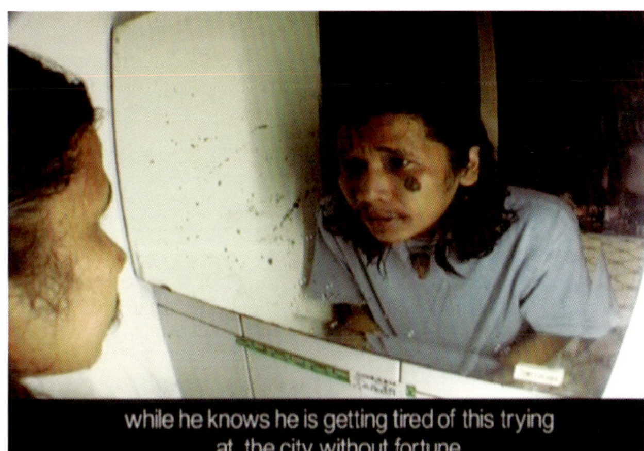
while he knows he is getting tired of this trying
at  the city without fortune.

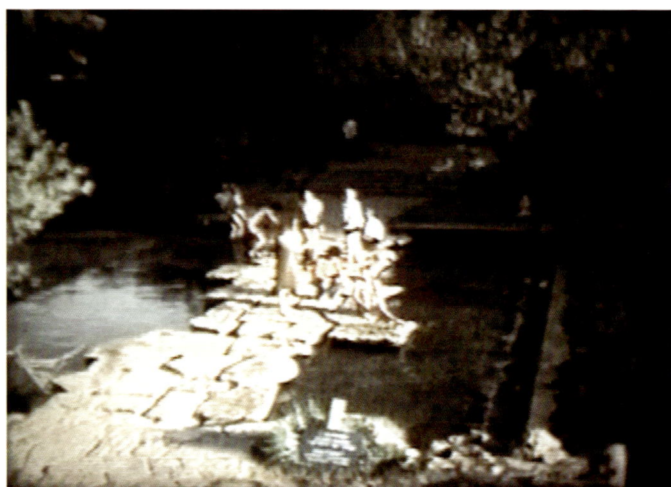

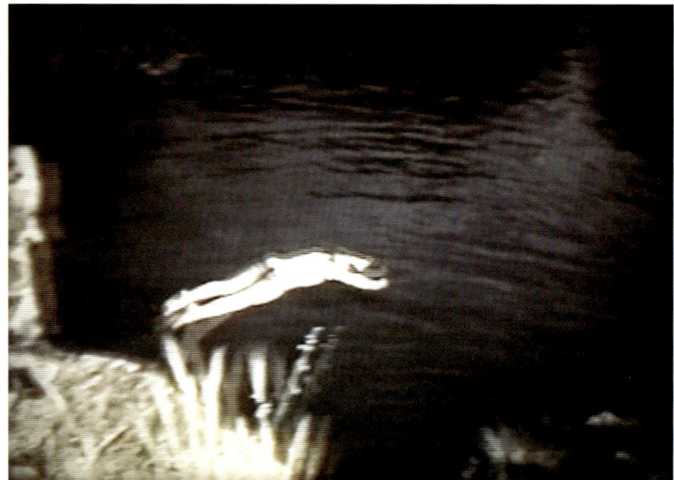

*Travel Agency,* 2001
VHS videotape on monitor
Courtesy of the artist

"I took super-8 shots that my father had taken in the '70s when we visited
our family who were spread out in Palestine/Israel. Scanning them gave me
the deep impression of looking at a more-than-lost world, as it already was
lost in the '70s. My father almost seemed to be branding images on the film
in a lovely, conserving way. I think he tried to look for a modern kind of
transferring of tradition… I tried to understand him while I was digging out
the old reels."

From a statement by the artist, 2001.

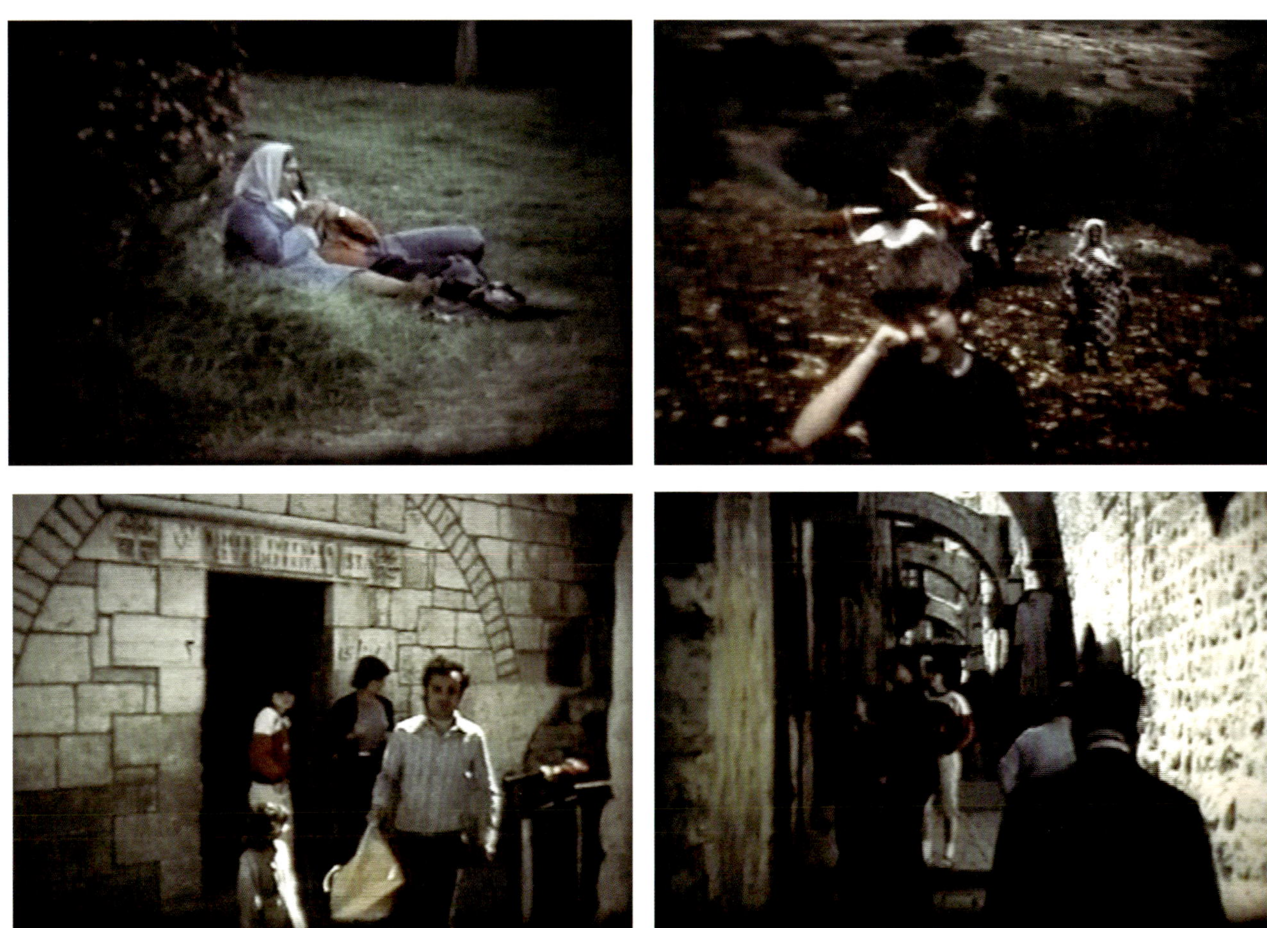

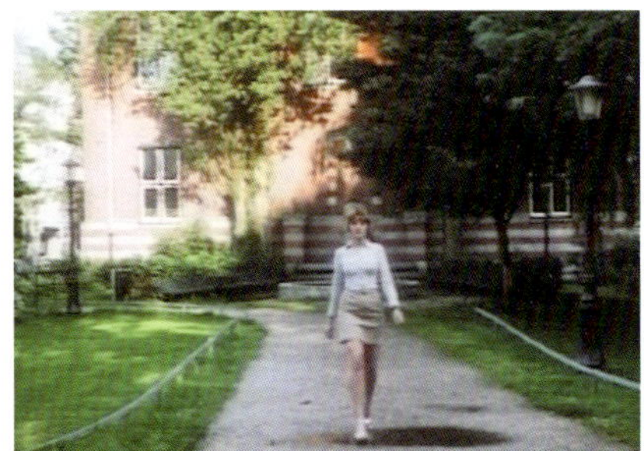 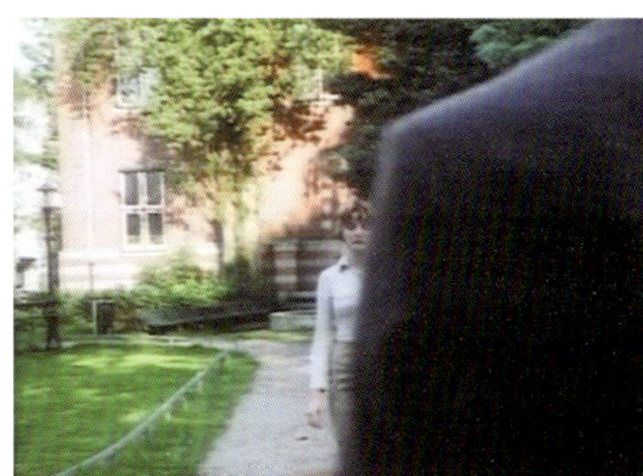 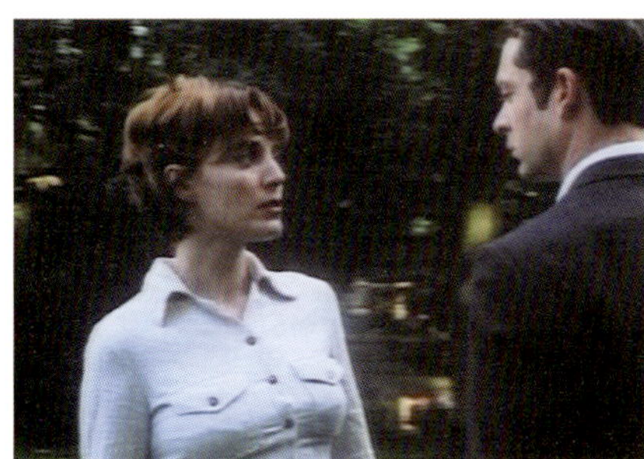

*Tuin*, 1998
2 DVD projections, 2 CDs, 16 mm film
Courtesy of Jay Jopling/White Cube, London

"The 360° track becomes a very important motif…. I think the moment in the film when the man eclipses the woman is very important, not necessarily for feminist reasons, but for any person whose identity has been overshadowed by another's."

See Runa Islam and David Bussel in *<hers> Video as a Female Terrain*, ed. Stella Rollig (New York: Springer-Verlag Wien, 2000).

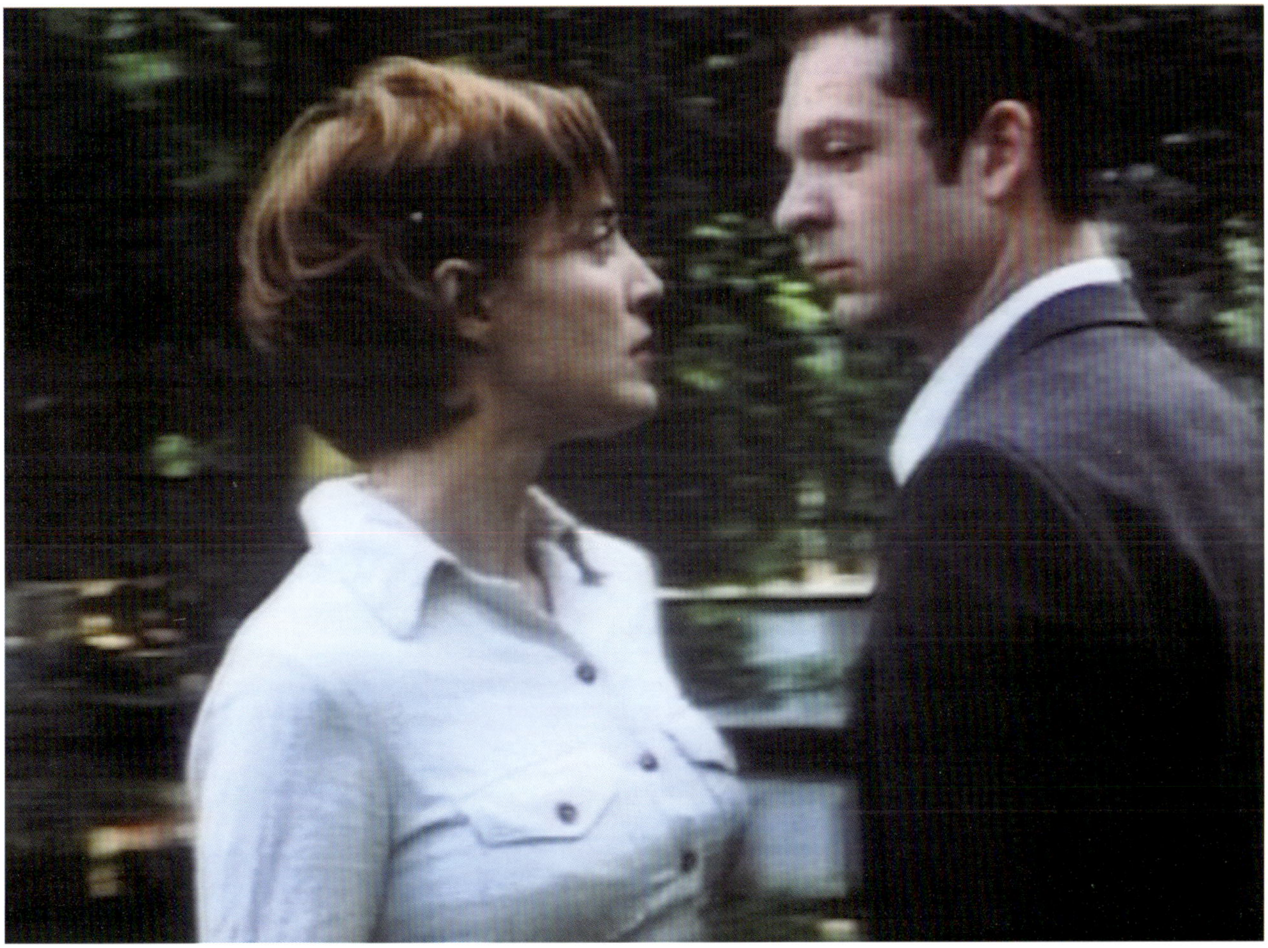

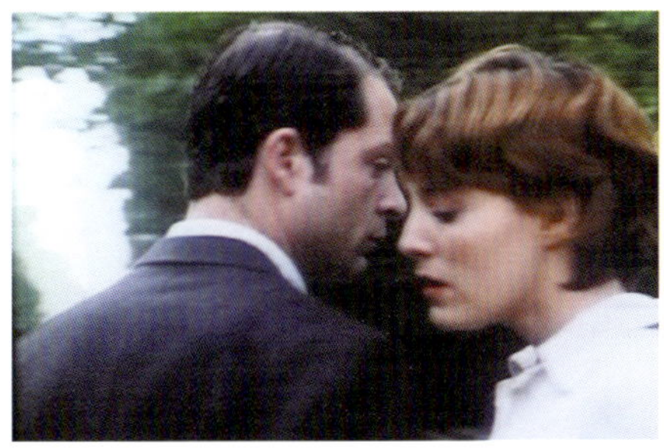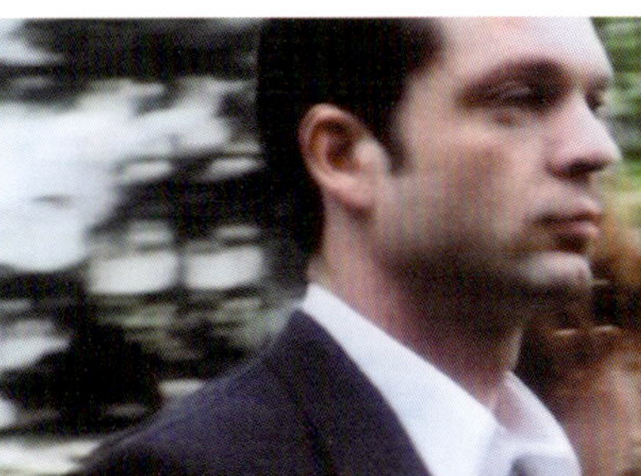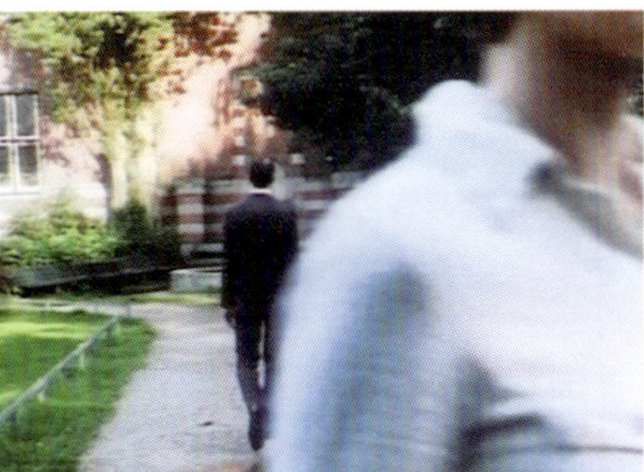

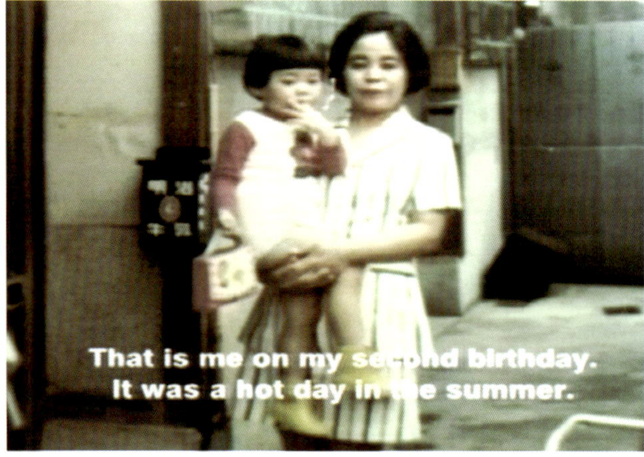


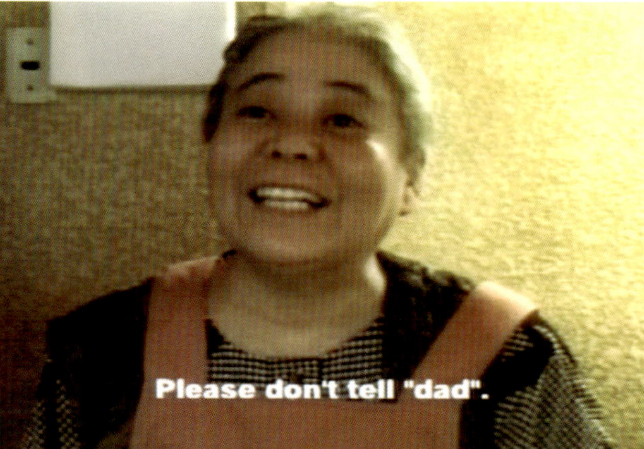


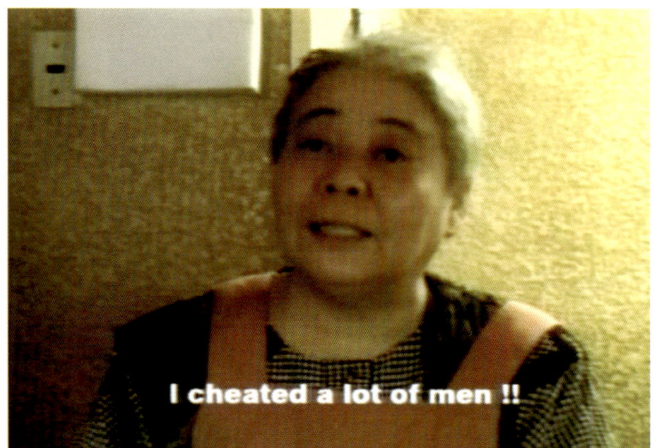


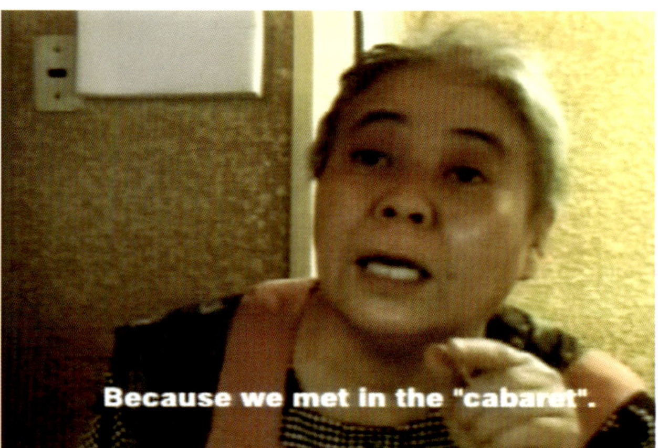


*Dutch Wife/Dutch Life*, 1996–2001
DVD projection
Courtesy of the artist

"I realize that if you talk about something the memory vanishes. That's
why I am only talking about the things around it."

From a statement by the artist, 2002.

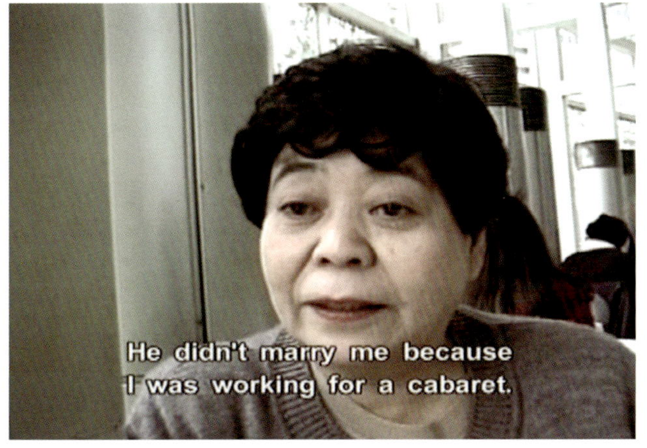
He didn't marry me because
I was working for a cabaret.

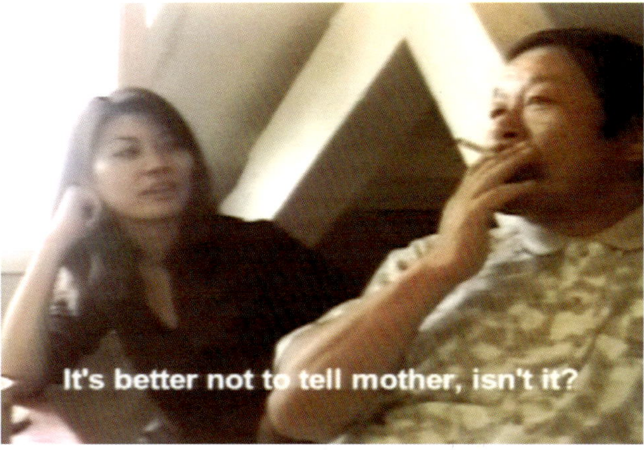
It's better not to tell mother, isn't it?

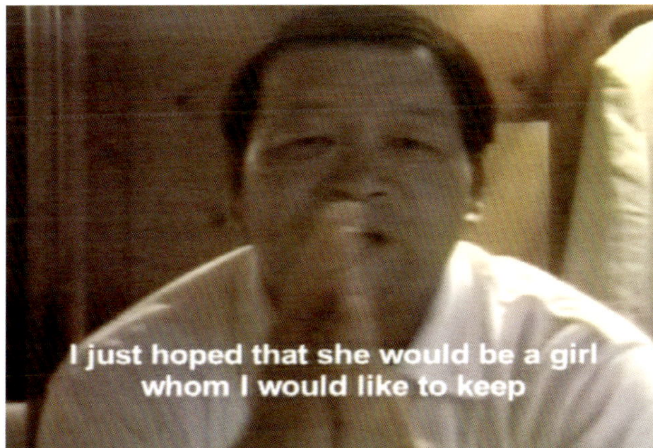
I just hoped that she would be a girl
whom I would like to keep

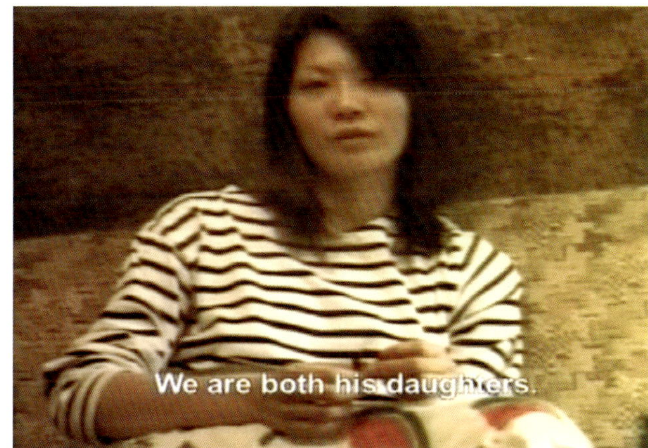
We are both his daughters.

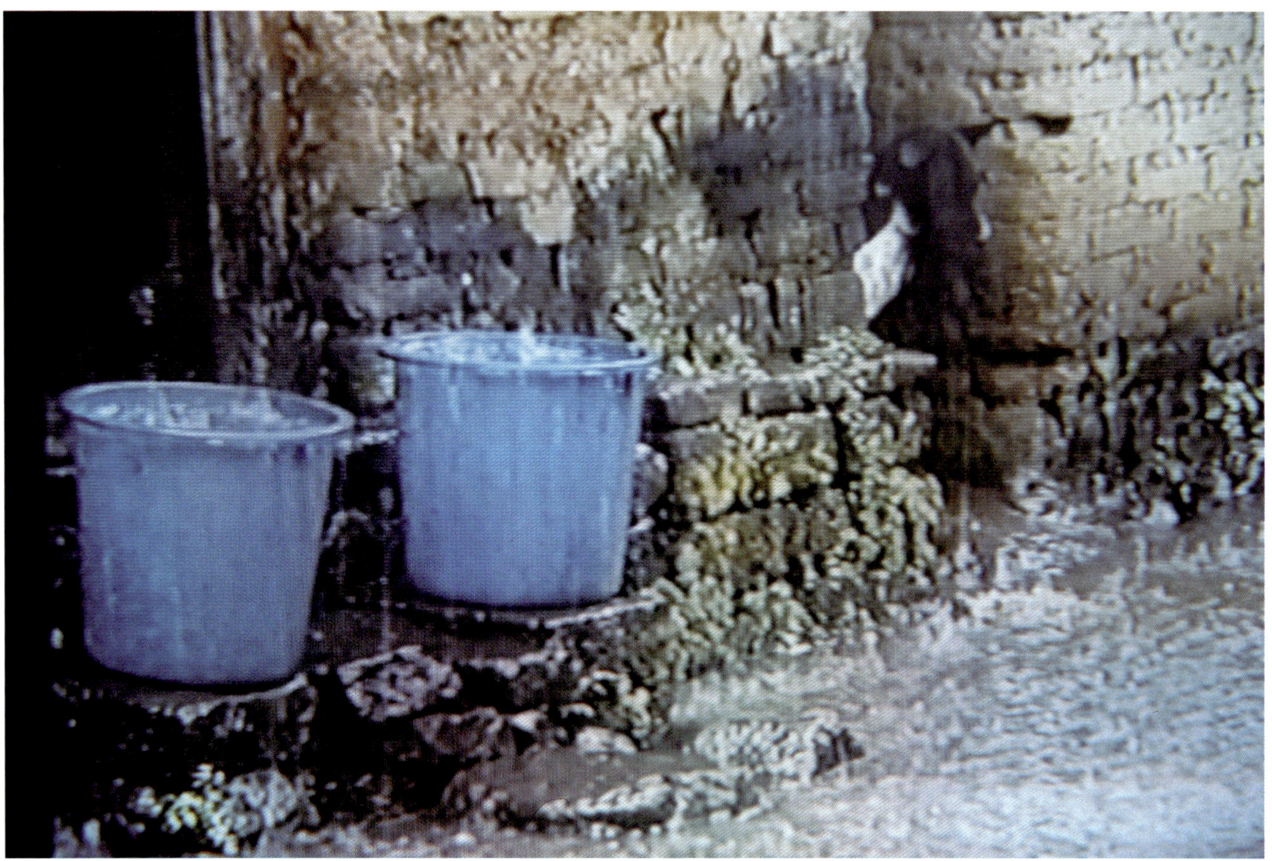

*Rain*, 2001
2 DVDs, 2 video monitors, metal brackets, shelves
Courtesy Galerie Paul Andriesse, Amsterdam

"It started off as a search, now it feels as if I'm constantly in
search of my search."

From a statement by the artist, as quoted by Lynn Cooke, "Fiona Tan: Re-Take,"
in Fiona Tan, *Scenario*. (Amsterdam: Vandenberg & Wallroth, 2000): 26.

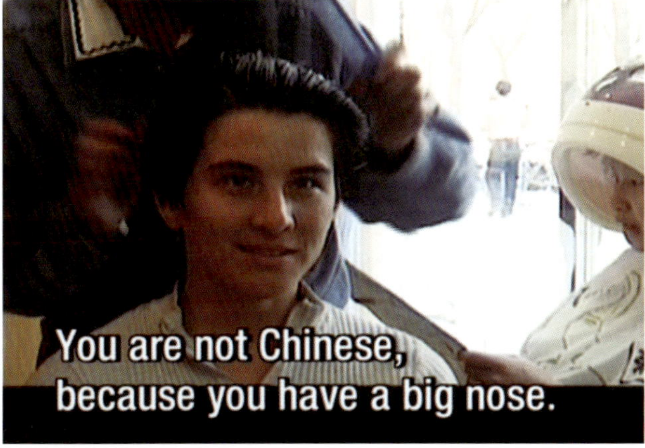

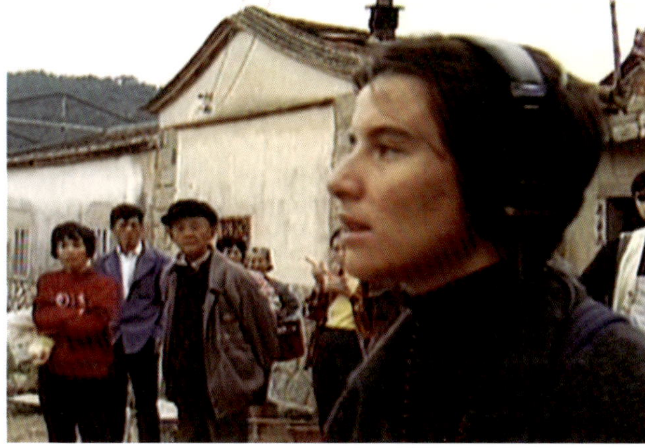
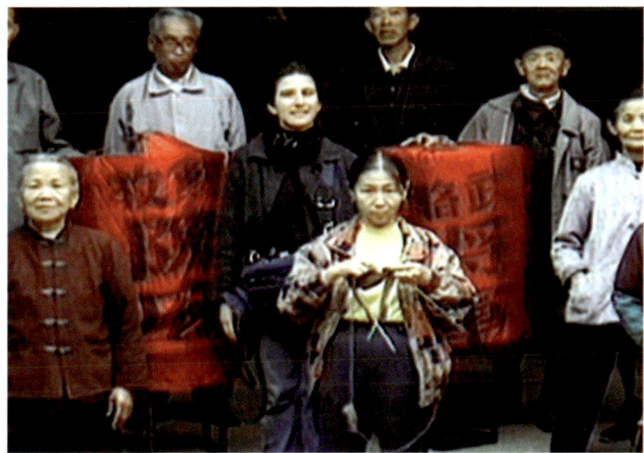
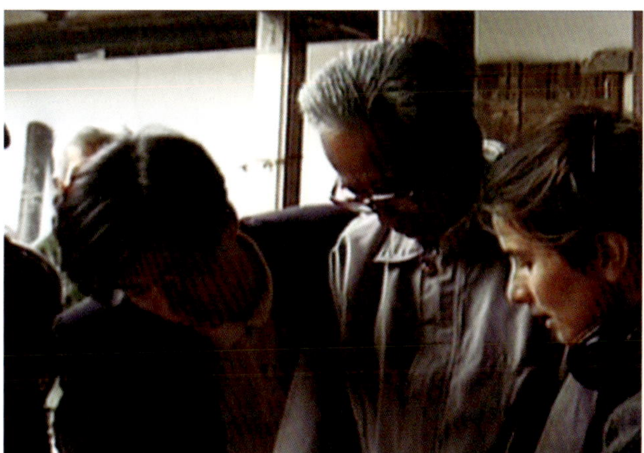

*May You Live in Interesting Times*, 1997
DVD projection
Courtesy Galerie Paul Andriesse, Amsterdam

# CARLOS AMORALES

Born in Mexico D.F. (Mexico City), Mexico, in 1970.
Lives and works in Amsterdam, The Netherlands, and Mexico City, Mexico

## EDUCATION/RESIDENCIES

2001 Ateliers des Artistes de la Ville de Marseille, France
Rijksakademie van Beeldende Kunsten, Amsterdam, The Netherlands
1992 Gerrit Rietveld Academie, Amsterdam, The Netherlands
–95

## SOLO EXHIBITIONS, SCREENINGS, PROJECTS

2002 *Fighting Evil (with style)*, University of South Florida Contemporary Art Museum, Tampa, FL, USA
*NEO (Near Earth Object)*, Ateliers des Artistes de la Ville de Marseille, France
*Sympathy for the Devil*, SKUC, Lubljana, Slovenia
2001 *CABARET AMORALES*, Migros Museum für Gegenwartskunst, Zurich, Switzerland
*Cuerpo sin alma, fotografía y video*, Galería Nina Menocal, Mexico City, Mexico
*Mexico City*, Mexico Video project, Montevideo/TBA, Amsterdam, The Netherlands
*Open*, Gallery Serge Ziegler, Zurich, Switzerland
2000 *Funny 13*, Galerie Micheline Szwajcer, Antwerp, Belgium
*Ideas for Living*, De Paviljoens, Almere, The Netherlands
*Los Mutantes/2 (collaboration with Michael Blum)*, Mexico City streets and El Caracol, Mexico City, Mexico
*A World All Too Familiar*, Center for Curatorial Studies, Bard College, Annandale-on-Hudson, NY, USA
1999 *As Amorales*, Galerie Fons Welters, Amsterdam, The Netherlands
*Infraslim*, Mayday Productions, New York, NY, USA
*Los Mutantes/1 (collaboration with Joan Jonas)*, Mexico City streets and El Caracol, Mexico City, Mexico
*Parking*, Mayday Productions, New York, NY, USA
*Project Room*, Museo Carrillo Gil, Mexico City, Mexico
*Stoplight Pastimes*, Marres Centrum, Maastricht, The Netherlands
1998 Galerie Micheline Szwajcer, Antwerp, Belgium
1997 *Amorales Interim*, Westergas Fabriek, Amsterdam, The Netherlands (performance)
*Arena dos de Mayo*, Arena Dos de Mayo, Cd. Neza, Mexico (performance)
*Amorales Table Dance*, W139, Amsterdam, The Netherlands (performance)
*Amorales in Conversation with...Superbarrio*, DeBalie, W139, Rijksakademie van Beeldende Kunsten, Amsterdam, The Netherlands
1996 *Anonymous Group Party (Zero)*, Rijksakademie van Beeldende Kunsten, Amsterdam, The Netherlands (performance)
*The Transparent Hide*, Rijksakademie van Beeldende Kunsten, Amsterdam, The Netherlands (performance)

## GROUP EXHIBITIONS

2002 *Living Like a Lover with a Radar Phone*, Project, Dublin, Ireland
*tele-journeys*, MIT List Visual Arts Center, Cambridge, MA, USA
2001 *House of Games*, Huis a/d Werf, Utrecht, The Netherlands
*Let's Entertain, (Kunst mach spass)*, Kunstmuseum Wolfsburg, Wolfsburg, Germany
*Mutation. La video mexicaine actuelle*, Ecole Supérieure des Beaux-Arts, Toulouse, France
*The Overexcited Body*, Museo del palazzo Arengario, Velodromo vogorelli, Milan; São Paolo, SESC Pompeia, Brazil
*Sport in der Zeitgenössischen Kunst*, Kunsthalle Nürnberg, Nürnberg, Germany
*Sportcult*, Apex Art, New York, NY, USA

Tiranna Biennale, National Gallery, Tiranna, Albania
*We in FLAMES*, 1.Berlin Biennale 2001, Berlin, Germany
2000 *inSITE 2000*, San Diego, CA, USA, and Tijuana, Mexico
*Let's Entertain*, Walker Art Center, Minneapolis, MN, USA; Portland Art Museum, Portland, OR, USA; (*Au dela du spectacle*), Musée national d'art moderne, Centre Georges Pompidou, Paris, France; Miami Art Museum, Miami, FL, USA
*Makeshift*, ArtPace, San Antonio, TX, USA
*Territorios Ausentes*, Casa de America, Madrid, Spain
*Unlimited NL–3*, De Appel, Amsterdam, The Netherlands
1999 *As Artist in Residence*, Foundation Artimo, Amsterdam, The Netherlands (online project)
*Peace*, Migros Museum für Gegenwartskunst, Zurich, Switzerland
1998 *Not Strictly Private*, Shed im Eisenwerk, Frauenfeld, Switzerland
*Faces and Names*, Exedra, Hilversum, The Netherlands
1997 *Niet de Kustvlaai*, Interim Performance, Westergas Fabriek, Amsterdam, The Netherlands

## BIBLIOGRAPHY


2001 Ellis, Patricia, Cuauhtemoc Medina, Philippe Vergne, Rein Wolfs, Carlos Amorales, Marco Rascon, Sebastian Lopez et al. —*los Amorales*. Amsterdam: Stichting Artimo, 2001.
2000 *Fresh Cream*. London: Phaidon Press, 2000.
*Ideas for Living*. Almere, The Netherlands: De Paviljoens, 2000.
*InSITE*. San Diego, CA, USA and Tijuana, Mexico: InSITE, 2000.
*Let's Entertain*. Mineapolis: Walker Art Center, 2000.
*Territorios Ausentes*. Madrid: Casa de America, 2000.
*Unlimited.nl–2*. Amsterdam: De Appel. 2000.
1999 *Amorales Interim*. Park TV (Berlin), 1999.
"Artist Contribution." *Material Magazine* (Zurich), November 1999.
"Entrevista con Amorales." *La Cultura Hoy*. Radio Universidad, (Mexico), 1999.
"Muestras de Emde y Amorales." *El Financiero* (Mexico), March 1999.
*Peace*. Zurich: Migros Museum für Gegenwartskunst, 1999.
"Tomas Emde y Carlos Amorales Exhibiran en el Carrillo Gil." *Excelsior* (Mexico), February 1999.
1998 HTV de Ijsberg, Amsterdam, The Netherlands, 1998.
Lambrecht, Luc. *De Morgen* (Antwerp), 1998.
*WIPE*, (New York), (November 1998).
Wyss, Dorine Abegg. "Junge Kunstler betrachten sich selbst: Not Strictly Private—Ausstellung im Eisenwerk-Shed." *Der Landbode* (Switzerland) 138, (1998).
Zwes, Annelise. "Auch bieler unter den jungen kuratoren." *Bieler Tagblatt* (Switzerland), (June 1998).
1997 *Amorales in Conversation with... Superbarrio*. HTV de Ijsberg, Amsterdam, The Netherlands, November 1997.
*Amorales Interim*. Amsterdam: W139 TV, 1997. (performance)
*Amorales Interim*. PARK 4AD TV, Amsterdam, The Netherlands, 1997.
Beijering, Sonja. *Dialogues*. Amsterdam, The Netherlands: W139, 1997.
Cabrera van Boeck, Fernando. "Superbarrio." *Revista Latina* (The Netherlands), (November 1997).
Gieben, Sabine. "Mexicaanse superhelden." *Elseviere* (The Netherlands), (October 1997).
*Super Powers*. Salto, The Netherlands: Almanac, 1997.
*Superbarrio*. Radio Amsterdam, October 1997.
*Superbarrio*. Radio Ikon (The Netherlands), October 1997.
*Superbarrio*. Red Radio Mundo (The Netherlands), October 1997.
"Superbarrio and Bishop Muskkens." *Nederland 3*, (1997).
van Royen, Marjon. "Held van de armen: buikje, cape en masker." *NRC Handelsblad* (Amsterdam), October 1997.


## ONLINE PROJECTS

1999 http://www.lostart.nl/amorales

**MARK BAIN**

Born in Seattle, WA, USA, in 1966
Lives and Works in Amsterdam, The Netherlands

**EDUCATION/RESIDENCIES**
2001    de Fabriek, Eindhoven, The Netherlands
1999    Rijksakademie van Beeldende Kunsten, Amsterdam, The
–00     Netherlands
1999    Massachusetts Institute of Technology, Cambridge, MA, USA
1998    Skowhegan School for Painting and Sculpture,
        Skowhegan, ME, USA
1990    School of the Art Institute of Chicago, Chicago, IL, USA
1986    Cornish College of Art, Seattle, WA, USA

**SOLO EXHIBITIONS, SCREENINGS, PROJECTS**
2001    *Feeler*, Cologne, Germany
        Galerie Romain Larivière, Paris, France
        *Resonating the Northern Avenue Bridge*, Boston Harbor, Boston,
        MA, USA
        *Stark Act of Removal*, Rooseum, Malmö, Sweden

**GROUP EXHIBITIONS, SCREENINGS, PROJECTS**
2002    *tele-journeys*, MIT List Visual Arts Center, Cambridge, MA, USA
2001    *Angel Machine*, Blue Moon Project—Mobile, Groningen,
        The Netherlands
        *Chair Show*, Udine, Italy
        *Crossflow*, Noord Zee Canal/Wijkertunnel, Velsen, The
        Netherlands
        *Disco for N/one*, Smart Project Space, Amsterdam, The
        Netherlands
        *Geo-Site: Portable Earthquake*, Fundament Foundation, Tilburg,
        The Netherlands
        *In the Meantime*, De Appel Foundation, Amsterdam, The
        Netherlands
        *Vibronic Listening Station*, Liste 01, Galerie Romain Larivière,
        Basel, Switzerland
2000    *Beacon*, NSA gallery, Durban, South Africa
        EXPO 2000, Global House Pavilion, Hanover, Germany
        Hedah Film Festival, Maastricht, The Netherlands
        *Open Ateliers*, Rijksakademie van Beeldende Kunsten,
        Amsterdam, The Netherlands
        *Rail Bridge*, Fuori Uso 2000, Pescara, Italy
        *Sense City for Viper*, Kunsthalle Basel, Basel, Switzerland
        *Wave Front*, Fort Lux, Fort Ijmuiden, The Netherlands
        *Three Industrial Landscape Recordings*, video/vibration installation
        *Venice*, Kunstvlaai 4/Impakt Festival, Amsterdam, The
        Netherlands
1999    *Field Recording, Tree Recording, Replicant, Office Projectile,*
        *The chair that leads outside my studio window*, Rijksakademie
        van Beeldende Kunsten, Amsterdam, The Netherlands
        *In Stabilities*, in European Media Arts Festival, Osnabrück,
        Germany; Lisbon Video Festival, Lisbon, Portugal
        *In Stabilities, The Recording Messenger*, Berlin Transmediale,
        Berlin, Germany
        *Soundtrack*, Laboratorium, Antwerp, Belgium
        *The Transient Vehicle*, Impakt, Utrecht, The Netherlands
        *X-SITE*, in *Anarchitecture*, De Appel Foundation, Amsterdam,
        The Netherlands
1998    *In Stabilities* in Muu Film and Video Festival, Helsinki, Finland;
        The International Festival of New Film and Video, Split, Croatia;
        16th World Wide Video Festival, Baby, Amsterdam, The
        Netherlands
        *The Live Room: Transducing Resonant Architecture* in Dutch
        Electronic Arts Festival (DEAF), V2, Rotterdam, The Netherlands
        *The Live Room*, Laboratory N51–117, Massachusetts Institute of
        Technology, Cambridge, MA, USA
        *Projectiles—Wall Star*, Building N51, Massachusetts

Institute of Technology, Cambridge, MA, USA
        *The Recording Messenger*, Viliegend Mannen, Goes,
        The Netherlands; Cut Copy Paradiso, Amsterdam,
        The Netherlands; 7th New York Video Festival,
        Lincoln Center, New York, NY, USA; 5th Mostra de
        Video Independent & Fenomens Interactius, Center de
        Cultura Contemporania de Barcelona, Barcelona, Spain;
        Impakt, Utrecht, The Netherlands
        *Rotodynamics in 3D, Filmform*, Stockholm, Sweden
        *The Vault*, Bank of Skowhegan, Skowhegan, ME, USA
        *The Vibronic Hut, The Vibronic Bridge*, Skowhegan
        School of Painting and Sculpture, Skowhegan, ME, USA
1997    *The Accelerator Project*, in Eventworks Festival,
        Massachusetts College of Art, Boston, MA, USA
        *Electrophase*, in 3e Manifestation International
        Vidéo et Art Electronique, Montréal, Québec, Canada; 4th
        Mostra de Video Independent & Fenomens Interactius, Center de
        Cultura Contemporania de Barcelona, Barcelona, Spain; and
        Vidéoforms 97, Clermont-Ferrand, France
        *Heaven: Public View-Private View*, still from *The Recording*, Long
        Island City, NY, USA
        *Re-Centering Geometer*, in *Seattle Arts Commission–Seattle Collects*
        *Seattle, Human References, Marks of the Artist* (a 10–year
        retrospective exhibition of the Seattle Artists' Program
        collection), Seattle Center Pavilion, Seattle, WA, USA
        *The Recording Messenger, Space Probing*, in Craig Baldwin's
        *The Artful Apparatus*, Artists Television Access (ATA) Gallery,
        San Francisco, CA, USA
        *The Recording Messenger*, in Film+arc-Graz, 3rd International
        Biennial of Film and Architecture, Graz, Austria;
        Videotage, Hong Kong, China; Eventworks Festival, Boston, MA,
        USA
        *Rotodynamics* in 3D, *Electrophase*, as part of touring show, *Other*
        *Cinema*, Perth Film and Video Festival, Film and Television
        Institute of Western Australia, Perth, Australia; and Royal
        Melbourne Institute of Technology and Erwin Rado Theatre,
        Melbourne, Australia
        *The Ventilator Project*, in *Repeat Reverse*, The Yale Art and
        Architecture Building Gallery, New Haven, CT, USA
1996    *Electrophase in Videonale 7*, Bonn, Germany; *Champ Libre, Sous*
        *La Passerelle!*, Montréal, Québec, Canada; *Video of the Nineties:*
        The International Festival of New Film and Video, Split, Croatia;
        5th New York Video Festival, Lincoln Center, New York, NY,
        USA; Impakt Festival, Utrecht, The Netherlands
1995    *Electrophase, Viper*, Lucerne, Switzerland; and in Cine-X Program:
        12th Annual Olympia Film Festival, Olympia, WA, USA
1994    *FLOATS: Derivations From a Cartecal Format of Reason*,
        Center on Contemporary Art (COCA), Seattle, WA, USA
        *The Noise Wall, Retinal Memory Induction, Texture Mapping*,
        La fou-art, Québec, Canada
        *Random Access*, Center on Contemporary Art (COCA), Seattle, WA,
        USA (*Interphase*—a collaboration with architect John Bain)
        *Two Untitled Machine Installations*, DAG/Division Artist Group,
        Chicago, IL, USA
        *Untitled Machine Installation*, BFA thesis exhibition,
        School of the Art Institute of Chicago, Chicago, IL, USA
1993    *Retinal Memory Induction, The Noise Wall*, Berlin Interfilm Festival,
        Berlin, Germany
        *Retinal Memory Induction*, Première Manifestation Internationale
        Vidéo et Art Electronique, Montréal, Québec, Canada
1992    *Retinal Memory Induction in The Best of Chine-X*, 911 Media Arts
        Center, Seattle, WA, USA
        *Mapping, Retinal Memory Induction in Perception And Our Machines*,
        Texture Seattle, WA, USA
        *Retinal Memory Induction*, The 9th Annual Olympia Film and Video
        Festival, WA, USA
        *Texture Mapping in Optical Explosions Show*, Chicago Filmmakers,
        Chicago, IL, USA

## AWARDS AND GRANTS

1999
–00
Rijksakademie van Beeldende Kunsten, Studium General Stipendium

1998
*The Live Room*, MIT Council for the Arts, Cambridge, MA, USA

1997
*The Ventilator Project*, MIT Council for the Arts, Cambridge, MA, USA

Canal+ Award, *Electrophase*, Vidéoforms 97, Clermont-Ferrand, France

Finalist: *Internationaler Videokunstpreis*, ZKM (Center for Media Art), Karlsruhe, Germany

1996
Seattle Artists Visual Arts Program commission, Seattle, WA, USA

1995
*22nd Northwest Film and Video Festival*, Judges' Selection Award, Portland, OR, USA

## BIBLIOGRAPHY

2001
Bain, Mark. "Soundtrack: Laboratorium." *Laboratorium*. Edited by Hans Ulrich Obrist and Barbara Vanderlinden. Antwerp: Dumont, 2001.

Ellis, Patricia. "Demolition Woman, Can I Be Your Man: Mark Bain," *World of Art*, (January 2001).

Rabertini, Alessandro. "Mark Bain." *Perchè*, (January 2001).

2000
Bain, Mark. "Mommy and I Are One." *In the Meantime*. Amsterdam: De Appel Foundation, 2001.

Bain, Mark. "Soundings for stationary objects (in to you like a train)." *The Bridges*. (Text by Andreas Schlegel.) Milan: Giancarlo Politi Editore, 2000.

Hankowitz, Molly and Cox, David. "Interview with Mark Bain." *M/C* (Australia), (September 2000).

1999
Bain, Mark. "The Speed of Architecture." *Anarchitecture*. Amsterdam: De Appel Foundation, 1999.

Bosma, Josephine. "Interview with Mark Bain." *Acoustic Space* (Latvia), (November 1999).

1998
Bain, Mark. "Thresholds 16, The Live Room: Transducing Resonant Architecture." *MIT Journal on Architecture* (Cambridge, MA, USA), (June 1998).

Nobel, Philip. "Ashes to Ashes, on the Ventilator Project." *Metropolis* (New York), (April 1998).

1996
Bain, Mark. "Thresholds 14, *Projectiles*." *MIT Journal on Architecture* (Cambridge, MA, USA), (June 1997).



# YAEL BARTANA

Born in Afula, Israel, in 1970
Lives and works in The Netherlands and Israel

## EDUCATION/RESIDENCIES

2001
Rijksakademie van Beeldende Kunsten, Amsterdam, The Netherlands

1999
School of Visual Arts, New York, NY, USA

1992
–96
The Bezalel Academy of Arts and Design, Jerusalem, Israel

## SOLO EXHIBITIONS

2002
*Trembling Time*, Beelden Aan Zee Museum, Scheveningen, The Netherlands

*variables X Y Z*, Digital Art Lab, Holon, Israel

2001
*Profile*, Caermersklooster, Ghent, Belgium

## GROUP EXHIBITIONS, SCREENINGS

2002
Gwangju Biennale, Gwangju, South Korea

31st International Film Festival Rotterdam, Rotterdam, The Netherlands

Manifesta 4, European Biennial of Contemporary Art, Frankfurt am Main, Germany

*Nonlinear Editing*, De Paviljoens, Almere, The Netherlands

*tele-journeys*, MIT List Visual Arts Center, Cambridge, MA, USA

*WHAT? A tale in free images*, Memlingmuseum, Brugge, Belgium (Culture Capital of Europe)

2001
*In the Mean Time*, De Appel, Amsterdam, The Netherlands

*Neue Welt*, Frankfurter Kunstverein, Frankfurt-am-Main, Germany

*Open Ateliers*, Rijksakademie van Beeldende Kunsten, Amsterdam, The Netherlands

2000
*Greater New York*, PS1, New York, NY, USA

*Open Ateliers*, Rijksakademie van Beeldende Kunsten, Amsterdam, The Netherlands

1997
*Mix New York City*, Film Festival, New York, NY, USA

1996
Experimental Film Festival Paris, Paris, France

## GRANTS/AWARDS

2001
Nuffic (The Netherlands Organization for International Cooperation in Higher Education), The Netherlands

2000
Stichting Schürmann-Krant, The Netherlands

Stichting Trustfonds Rijksakademie, Amsterdam, The Netherlands

1996
Bezalel Academy of Art and Design, Jerusalem, Israel

## BIBLIOGRAPHY



2001
den Hartog Jager, Hans. "Keelzangers en een dood paard in Open Ateliers." *NRC Handelsblad* (The Netherlands), 2001.

Mar, Alex. "In the Meantime...." *Metropolis M*, (summer 2001): 48.

Moukhtar, Esma. "Boodschappen in een trillingslaag." *de Volkskrant* (The Netherlands), 2001.

van de Velde, Paola. "Marsmuziek en een leger van naalden. Amsterdamse Rijksakademie houdt Open Ateliers." *De Telegraaf* (Amsterdam, The Netherlands), 2001.

2000
de Vries, Marina. "Liever een camera dan verf en kwast." *Het Parool* (Amsterdam, The Netherlands), 2000.

"Geluid, veel geluid in Open Ateliers." *de Volkskrant* (The Netherlands), 2000.

Lamoree, Jhim. "Veel installaties en een enkel schilderij of beeld." *Het Parool* (Amsterdam, The Netherlands), 2000.

van de Velde, Paola. "Jennifer Tee serveert taart. Rijksakademie-studenten hebben overduidelijk lol in hun werk." *De TeLegraaf* (Amsterdam, The Netherlands), 2000.



# MICHAEL BLUM

Born in Jerusalem, Israel, in 1966
Lives and works in Paris, France

## EDUCATION/RESIDENCIES

2001
Ruang Rupa, Jakarta, Indonesia

2000
–01
Rijksakademie van Beeldende Kunsten, Amsterdam, The Netherlands

1998
Banff Centre for the Arts, Banff, Alberta, Canada

1997
Glasgow School of Art, Glasgow, Scotland

1992
École Nationale de la Photographie, Arles, France

1988
University of Paris Panthéon-Sorbonne, Paris, France

## SOLO EXHIBITIONS, SCREENINGS, PROJECTS

2002
*Kunstkanaal*, Amsterdam, Rotterdam, Den Haag, The Netherlands

2000
Der Standard, Vienna, Austria

*Homo Œconomicus*, Stanley-Picker Gallery, Kingston-upon-Thames, UK

Museum in Progress, 30.11 www.mip.at/en/werke/474.html

1998
*Tales of Britain*, Espace Culturel François Mitterand, Beauvais, France

*Vacance, Venividi*, Shopping Center, Ivry-sur-Seine, France

1997
*C'est la vie, au rendez-vous des clowns*, Galerie Elisabeth Valleix, Paris, France

*La salle des temps perdus*, le Grand Wazoo, Amiens, France

*Un rude hiver*, Musée des Beaux-Arts et de la Dentelle, Calais, France

1996
*De deux choses l'une*, le Grand Wazoo, Amiens, France

Virtual Actions, www.icono.org/virtual/actions.htm

**GROUP EXHIBITIONS, SCREENINGS, PROJECTS**

2002  *BIG*, Torino, Italy
Galerie Thaddaeus Ropac, Paris, France
*Non-Places*, Frankfurter Kunstverein, Frankfurt am Main, Germany
*tele-journeys*, MIT List Visual Arts Center, Cambridge, MA, USA

2001  *58 films cash*, Musée d'art contemporain, Marseille, France
*Broadway*, Paris de l'hotel de ville, Paris, France CBK/TENT, Rotterdam, The Netherlands
*Den-city*, Eme3/CCCB, Barcelona, Spain
Festival internacional de musica contemporanea, Maloka Imax Cinema, Bogota, Columbia
*Going places*, Smart Project Space, Amsterdam, The Netherlands
Hamburger Kammerkunstverein, Hamburg, Germany
*Open Ateliers*, Rijksakademie van Beeldende Kunsten, Amsterdam, The Netherlands
Park 4DTV, Amsterdam, The Netherlands
Salto 1 TV, Amsterdam, The Netherlands
*Take Two/Reprise*, Ottawa Art Gallery, Ottawa, Ontario, Canada

2000  *6e Vidéogrammes*, Marseille, France
Contribution to Simon Morris' *Bibliomania*, www.bibliomania.org.uk
*Crash*, www.sidestreet.org/sitestreet/
*I.C.I.*, W139, Amsterdam, The Netherlands
*The Language Course* (collaboration with Carlos Amorales), El Caracol, Mexico City, Mexico
*Open Ateliers*, Rijksakademie van Beeldende Kunsten, Amsterdam, The Netherlands
*Public Inventions and Interventions*, Temporary Services, Chicago, IL, USA
*Videoszene Paris*, Konstruirte Wirklichkeit, Huis a/d Werf, Utrecht, The Netherlands
Viper Festival, Basel, Switzerland
18th World Wide Video Festival, Amsterdam, The Netherlands

1999  *28e festival du nouveau cinéma et des nouveaux medias*, Montréal, Québec, Canada
Bandits-Mages, Bourges, France
*But is it politics?* www.lot.or.at/politics/index.htm (website by Sabine Bitter and Helmut Weber)
Kunstmuseum des Kantons Thurgau, Warth, Switzerland
*Events/Ipso Facto*, Galerie Yvon Lambert, Paris, France
Ipso Facto, Nantes, France
*Rentrée*, Stanley-Picker Gallery, Kingston-upon-Thames, UK
Rue Marcel Duchamp, Paris, France
*V Tape*, Toronto, Canada, www.vtape.org
*Videoszene Paris*, Konstruirte Wirklichkeit, Kunsthalle, Basel, Switzerland
*Visions Underground*, Stalingrad Métro Station, Paris, France

1998  The Banff Centre for the Arts, Banff, Alberta, Canada
*Disquieting Strangeness*, Centre for Freudian Analysis and Research, London, UK
*Glassbox Open*, Glassbox, Paris, France
*Une histoire de circonstances*, Le Lieu, Lorient, France
Librairie Florence Loewy, Paris-Photo Fair, Paris, France
*Vidéochroniques*, Marseilles, France

1997  *Happy Hour*, Galerie Elisabeth Valleix, FIAC, Paris, France
*N° 5, Casa Factori*, public posting in Marseilles/Paris, France, Leipzig, Germany, Casablanca, Morocco
*Sous le manteau*, Galerie Thaddaeus Ropac, Paris, France
*Venividi*, SAGA, Paris, France

1996  *9e Instants Vidéo*, Manosque, France
*Les cent jours d'art contemporain*, Centre international d'art contemporain de Montréal (CIAC), Montréal, Québec, Canada
*Marché de Noël*, 81 rue Albert, Paris, France
*Thés Vidéo/La Revue Éclair*, Galerie EOF, Paris, France

1995  *Le couvert est mis*, Zoo Galerie, Nantes, France
*Voisins et amis*, À l'Écart, Montreuil, France

1994  *08 316 794*, L'Embarcadère, Lyon, France
*Comment raser un donjon qui dérange?*, À l'Écart, Montreuil, France

1993  *One-Minute Festival*, São Paulo, Brazil

1992  *A Bao A Qou*, EPE, Paris, France
*Image de soi/image d'autrui*, Greniers de César, Amboise, France

1991  *Travaux en cours*, XXIIe RIP, Arles, France

**PUBLIC COLLECTIONS**

City of Beauvais France; Depot, Vienna, Austria; Fonds National d'Art Contemporain, Paris, France; Musée national d'art moderne, Centre Georges-Pompidou, Paris, France

**GRANTS/AWARDS**

2001  The Ministry of Culture, Education and Science, The Netherlands
AFAA/DAP, France

2000  Stichting Schürmann-Krant, Amsterdam, The Netherlands

1999  Prix du FRAC Île-de-France, Paris, France

1998  DRAC Île-de-France, The Ministry of Culture, France

1994  City of Paris, France
DRAC Île-de-France, The Ministry of Culture, France

1993  Research grant, Mission du Patrimoine Photographique, Paris, France

**BIBLIOGRAPHY**

2001  Bronwasser, Sacha. "Op hol geslagen legioen in vloeibaar zand." *De Volkskrant* (The Netherlands), 30 November 2001.
Blum, Michael. *Cabinet* (Immaterial Incorporated) (New York, NY, USA) 3, (2001).
Faguet, Michèle. "The Fear of Returning and Being Misunderstood." *Parachute* 104, (2001): 125.
"Icono.org." *Le journal du CNP* 14, (2001).
Groot, M. "Kunstenaars Rijksakademie tonen eigen werk." *Noordhollandse Dagblad*, 30 November 2001.
Blum, Michael. potlatch.doc <printed matter for waiting room> ISBN 2–9515349–1–4
*Silent Zones—on Globalization and Cultural Interaction*. Amsterdam: RABK, 2001, 64–67.

2000  Blum, Michael. *Homo Œconomicus*. Amsterdam: De Balie/IDEA Books, 2000.
Blum, Michael. "L'irréductible substance." *Journal of The Centre For Freudian Analysis and Research*, (special issue 2000).
Blum, Michael. *Trece Respuestas*, La Revista del CGAC 0, Santiago de Compostela, Spain
*The Network*. Stockport, United Kingdom: Dewi Lewis Publishing, 2000.
de Groot, Anita. "Wandering Marxwards." *World Wide Video Festival*, 2000.
"Food for thought." *ArchiNed* (The Netherlands), 20 November 2000. www.ArchiNed.nl

1999  *Aden 70*, (31 March 1999).
Blum, Michael. "Translocal Poll." *Zéro Deux* 9, (April 1999).
Gicquel, Pierre. "Des rencontres imprévisibles." *Ouest-France*, 9 (April 1999).
*L'image, le monde* (Liège) 1, (1999).

1998  de Saint-Fare, Eric. "Les Contes de Monsieur Blum." *DDO* 33, (July 1998).

1997  "L'atelier, François Mitaine." Radio FG (Paris), 16 March 1997.
Blum, Michael. *La salle des temps perdus*. Amiens: Le Grand Wazoo, 1997.
Demir, Anaïd. "L'art fait le lit de la mode." *Technikart* (France), (March 1997).
"Michael Blum en attente." *Le courier picard* (Amiens, France), 17 January 1997.
"Michael Blum à la recherche du temps perdu." *Le courier picard* (Amiens, France), 22 January 1997.
Nguyen, Thuy-Diep. "Sous le manteau." *Le journal des expositions*, (April 1997).
"Réalité virtuelle: quel oxymoron!" (self-interview). *Oui* (France) 2, (1997).

1996 *Le courier picard*, (Amiens, France), 14 February 1995.
de la Broise. Tristan and Félix Torres. *Schneider, l'Histoire en Force*.
Paris: Editions de Monza, 1996. (Michael Blum contributed
historical research on industrial photography, 19th and 20th
centuries.)
Mercier, Marc. "Figures libres." *BREF 31*, (November 1996).

1995 "Zwickau zappelt als "Z" im Pariser Netz." *Die Freie Presse*,
(Zwickau), 7 July 1995.

## SEBASTIAN DIAZ MORALES

Born in Comodoro Rivadavia, Chubut, Argentina, in 1975
Lives and works in Amsterdam, The Netherlands

### EDUCATION/RESIDENCIES
2001 Rijksakademie van Beeldende Kunsten,
Amsterdam, The Netherlands
1993 Universidad del Cine de Antin, Capital Federal,
–99 Argentina

### SOLO EXHIBITIONS, SCREENINGS, PROJECTS
2002 *Complilation of Works from Just Like a That Productions*,
Museum Abteiberg, Mönchengladbach, Germany
2001 Trip from Amsterdam to Paris on a found boat called "La Cultura"
2000 *Open Circuit* (collaboration with Jo Ractliffe),
NSA Gallery, Durban, South Africa
1999 *Mural Instantaneo*, Comodoro Rivadavia, Chubut, Argentina
*Latin-American Filmmakers*, New York, NY, USA
1998 Cine Teatro Espanhol, Comodoro Rivadavia, Argentina
*Newer Collective Shorts*, Portland, OR, USA
1997 Cine Teatro Espanhol, Comodoro Rivadavia, Chubut, Argentina

### GROUP EXHIBITIONS, SCREENINGS, PROJECTS
2002 25th Bienal Internacional de São Paolo, São Paolo, Brazil
International Film Festival of Rotterdam, Rotterdam, The
Netherlands
RAIN Artists' Initiative, Network, *El Despacho Workshop*, Mexico
City, Mexico
*tele-journeys*, MIT List Visual Arts Center, Cambridge, MA, USA
2001 Impakt Festival, Centraal Museum, Utrecht, The Netherlands
*In the Meantime*, 2.Biennial Berlin, Berlin, Germany;
Museo Nacional Centro de Arte Reina Sofía, Madrid,
Spain; De Balie, Amsterdam, The Netherlands; De Appel,
Amsterdam, The Netherlands
*Open Ateliers*, Rijksakademie van Beeldende Kunsten,
Amsterdam, The Netherlands
*One Year Later* (collaboration with Jo Ractliffe), Joubert
Park Project, Johannesburg, South Africa
RAIN Artists' Initiative Network, Ruang Rupa Workshop, Jakarta,
Indonesia
*Silent Forces*, Hall Pusat Kebudayaan Jepang, Jakarta, Indonesia
19th World Wide Video Festival, Melkweg and W139,
Amsterdam, The Netherlands
2000 *Argentina* (Installation in collaboration with Patricio
Larrambebere), Rijksakademie van Beeldende Kunsten,
Amsterdam, The Netherlands
Independent Film and Video Festival, New York Film
Academy, New York, NY, USA
PICAF (Pusan International Contemporary Art Festival),
Pusan, South Korea
RAIN Artists' Initiative Network, *Pulse Workshop*, Durban,
South Africa
Tiempos Cortos Festival, Buenos Aires, Argentina
18th World Wide Video Festival, Melkweg and W139,
Amsterdam, The Netherlands

1999 *Cien Anhos y un Mes (Homenaje a Jorge Luis Borges)*,
Buenos Aires, Argentina
17th World Wide Video Festival, Melkweg and W139,
Amsterdam, The Netherlands
1998 Buenos Aires No Duerme Festival, Buenos Aires, Argentina
*ECOVISION*, Mar del Plata, Argentina
Tiempos Cortos Festival, Buenos Aires, Argentina
1997 Buenos Aires No Duerme Festival, Buenos Aires, Argentina
Imagine Leggera Video Festival, Palermo, Italy
*Premio ICI de Video*, Buenos Aires, Argentina
Tiempos Cortos Festival, Buenos Aires, Argentina
15th World Wide Video Festival, Melkweg, and Stedelijk
Museum Bureau Amsterdam, Amsterdam, The Netherlands
1996 F.I.V. International Video Festival, Buenos Aires, Argentina

### AWARDS
2001 11th Van Bommel Van Dam prijs, Museum Van Bommel
Van Dam, Venlo, The Netherlands
2000 "Best Experimental Feature Movie" Independent Film
and Video Festival, New York Film Academy, New York, NY, USA
1998 "Best Editing for a Documentary," Festival de Video de
Cordoba, Cordoba, Argentina
Special awards *La Tribu, Nuevas Miradas* and *DERHUMALC*
(Derechos Humanos y Medio Ambiente, America Latina y El
Caribe), Buenos Aires, Argentina
1997 Second Prize, Fin de Siglo Festival, ORT Institute,
Buenos Aires, Argentina
1995 First Prize, Video Poem Festival, Comodoro Rivadavia,
Chubut, Argentina

### BIBLIOGRAPHY
2001 Van Dam prijs. Venlo, The Netherlands: Museum Van Bommel
Van Dam, 2001.
*In The Meantime*. Amsterdam: De Appel, 2001.
*KARBON*. Jakarta, Indonesia: Ruang Rupa Workshop, 2001.
*Open Circuit*. NSA Gallery, Durban, South Africa: NSA Gallery,
2001.
*World Wide Video Festival*. Amsterdam: Melkweg and W139, 2001.
2000 *PICAF (Pusan International Contemporary Art Festival)*. Pusan, South
Korea: Pusan International Contemporary Art Festival, 2000.
*World Wide Video Festival*. Amsterdam: Melkweg and W139, 2000.
1999 *World Wide Video Festival*. Amsterdam: Melkweg and W139, 1999.
1997 *World Wide Video Festival*. Amsterdam: Melkweg, and Stedelijk
Museum Bureau Amsterdam, 1997.
*Immagine Leggera*. Palermo, Italy: Immagine Leggera Video
Festival, 1997.

### BROADCASTS
2001 *15,000,000 Parachutes* on Kunst Kanaal. Amsterdam, The
Netherlands
*The Persecution of the White Car* on Kunst Kanaal. Amsterdam, The
Netherlands
1997 Various Broadcasts on Argentinean Cable Channels
–99

### WEB PAGES
*www.unionquilimbay.freeservers.com* (Production Company)
*www.lacultura.com* (Boat Project Amsterdam Paris)
*www.argentinie.freeservers.com* (Installation with Patricio Larrambebere)

### REVIEWS AND PROGRAMS ON WEB PAGES
*www.artthrob.co.za/01mar/reviews.html*
*www.artthrob.co.za/01feb/listings-kzn.html#nsa2*
*www.wwvf.nl/18/programme/0diaz.htm*
*www.wwvf.nl/17/program/artists/0moralesx.htm*
*www.unionquilimbay.freeservers.com*

**NABILA IRSHAID**

Born in Osnabrück, Germany, in 1964
Lives and works in Salzburg, Austria

**EDUCATION/RESIDENCIES**
1993    Hochschule für Bildende Künste (HfBK), Hamburg, Germany
–99

**SOLO EXHIBITIONS, SCREENINGS, PROJECTS**
2001    Galerie Art Projects, Vilnius, Lithuania
1998    Metropolis Cinema, Hamburg, Germany

**GROUP EXHIBITIONS, SCREENINGS, PROJECTS**
2002    Salzburger Kunstverein, Salzburg, Austria
        *Stalactites*, Otto Gallery, Munich, Germany
        *tele-journeys*, MIT List Visual Arts Center, Cambridge, MA, USA
2001    *handcatcher and soft traps*, Rampe Gallery, Bielefeld, Germany
        Internet Project, Border Hacking Congress, Mexico
        *ORF, Kunststücke*, Austrian Television, Vienna, Austria
        Salzburger Kunstverein, Salzburg, Austria
        *Summeracademy*, Salzburg, Austria
1999    Advertising Office Beierarbeit, Bielefeld, Germany
        Gallery Tiefensee, Rinteln, Germany
        Metropolis Cinema, Hamburg, Germany
1997    *Vases*, Gallery Tiefensee, Rinteln, Germany
        Lightboxes for the City of Hamburg, Freundeskreis der
        Hochschule für Bildende Künste (HfBK) Hamburg, Germany
1996    Ars Electronica, Linz, Austria
        Digital Art Gallery, Frankfurt, Germany
        Elida Fabergé Competition, Munchen Film Fest, Munich,
        Germany
        Filmtage, Hannover, Germany
        ShortFilmFestival, Hamburg, Germany
1994    Ars Electronica, Linz, Austria
        *ORF, Kunststücke*, Austrian Television, Vienna, Austria
        Metropolis Cinema, Hamburg, Germany
        Nordstadt Film Days, Hannover, Germany
        Salzburger Kunstverein, Salzburg, Austria
        *Ship of Media*, Stubnitz: St. Petersburg, Russia, Vienna, Austria,
        Hamburg, Germany
        ShortFilmFestival, Hamburg, Germany

**OTHER**
2001    Purchase, Government of Austria, BKA for the Residence,
        Salzburg, Austria
1997    Independent video production in cooperation with
        Abbildungszentrum Hamburg, Germany
1995    Scholarship, Sammelstiftung der Hochschule für Bildende Künste
        (HfBK), Hamburg, Germany


**RUNA ISLAM**

Born in Dhaka, Bangladesh, in 1970
Lives and works in London, UK

**EDUCATION**
1997    Rijksakademie van Beeldende Kunsten, Amsterdam, The
–98     Netherlands
1995    Middlesex University, Middlesex, UK
        Manchester Metropolitan University, Manchester, UK

**SOLO EXHIBITIONS**
2001    *Director's Cut (Fool for Love)*, White Cube, London, UK
        *One day a day will come when a day will not come anymore*, April,
        in parking meters in Cologne, Germany
2000    *Screen Test/Unscript*, Fig–1, London, UK

**GROUP EXHIBITIONS, SCREENINGS**
2002    *tele-journeys*, MIT List Visual Arts Center, Cambridge, MA, USA
2001    *Black Cube 6. Film en video, installaties en performances*, Cinema de
        Balie, Amsterdam, The Netherlands
        *Century City*, Tate Modern, London, UK
        *Cité* (with Roger Cremers), Institute Hollandaise, Paris, France
        *Crylawn Art 11*, California Institute of Technology, Pasadena, CA,
        USA
        *Foot Loose*, Stedelijk Museum Bureau Amsterdam, Amsterdam,
        The Netherlands
        *Gymnasion*, Bregenzer Kunstverein, Bregenz, Austria
        *Hedah Film Festival*, Maastricht, The Netherlands
        *Idea Festival, Video in the City*, Centrum Hedendaagse Kunst,
        Maastricht, The Netherlands.
        *In/SITE/out. Inquiries into Social Space*, Apex Art, New York, NY, USA
        *Looking With/Out*, Courtauld Institute, London, UK
        *Neue Welt*, Frankfurter Kunstverein, Frankfurt am Main, Germany
        *Please Disturb Me*, Great Eastern Hotel, London, UK
        *Squatters*, Museu de Serralves, Oporto, Portugal; Witte de with,
        Rotterdam, The Netherlands
        *Video*, Barbara Gross Galerie, Munich, Germany
        *What's Wrong* (with Peter Lewis), Trade Apartment, London, UK
        *The Whitechapel Centenary*, Whitechapel, London, UK
2000    *Alice in Bed* by Susan Sontag (with HZT and New York
        Theatre Workshop), New York, NY, USA
        *And If There Were No Stories*, Stephen Friedman Gallery, London,UK
        *The British Art Show*, South Bank Centre (touring exhibition:
        Edinburgh, Southampton, and Cardiff, UK)
        *Devil Eats Out*, Flag, London, UK
        *Guarene Arte 2000*, Palazzo Re Rebaudengo, Guarene d'Alba, Italy
        Haven Lodge Residential Home, Ramsgate, UK
        *<hers> Video as a Female Terrain*, Steirischerherbst Landesmuseum,
        Joanneum, Graz, Austria
        *History Lessons*, Kunst en der Stadt 2000, (with Peter Lewis),
        Korn Theatre, Bregenz, Austria
        *Nurture and Desire* (in Aid of Breakthrough Breast Cancer),
        Hayward Gallery, London, UK
        *Point of View*, Richard Salmon, London, UK
        *Sublime*, Duende, Rotterdam, The Netherlands
        *Wouldn't it Be Nice*, Montevideo/TBA, Amsterdam, The
        Netherlands
1999    *000zerozerozero*, Whitechapel Art Gallery, London, UK
        *Amnesiac Cinema*, Galerie du Bellay, Mont-St-Aijan, France
        *Dis.Location*, hARTware projekte, Dortmund, Germany
        East International, Norwich Art Gallery, Norwich, UK
        Masterclass 1999, KHM, Cologne, Germany
        *Ninenineninetynine*, Anthony Wilkinson Gallery, London, UK
        *Open Electronic Festival*, USVA, Groningen, The Netherlands
        *Runa Islam*, Tschumi Pavilion, Groninger Museum, Groningen,
        The Netherlands
        *Runa Islam* at Impakt Festival, Begane Grond, Utrecht, The
        Netherlands
        *Stimuli*, Witte de With, Rotterdam, The Netherlands
        *Voor Bij De Realiteit*, SuB-K, Utrecht, The Netherlands
        17th World Wide Video Festival, Stedlijk Museum Bureau
        Amsterdam, The Netherlands
1998    *Beloved, The Waiting Room*, Wolverhampton, UK
        *Host*, Tramway, Glasgow, Scotland
        *Martin*, Catalyst Arts, Belfast, Northern Ireland, and Waygood
        Gallery, Newcastle, UK
        *Near*, Sharzah Museum of Art, Sharzah, United Arab Emirates
        *Open Ateliers*, Rijksakademie van Beeldende Kunsten, Amsterdam,
        The Netherlands
        *Plaats* (with J. Daf, P. Fillingham and J. Issacs), W139,
        Amsterdam, The Netherlands
        *The Road*, Espace Culturel François Mitterand, Beauvais, France
        *Scope*, Artists Space, New York, NY, USA

*The Vauxhall Gardens*, Norwich Art Gallery, Norwich, UK
1997 *Big Blue*, Coins, London, UK, and Café Fix, Berlin, Germany
*Colo(u)rblind*, Salle de Bains, Rotterdam, The Netherlands
*Curator's Arse* (with Peter Lewis) Martin, Catalyst Arts, Belfast
Northern Ireland, and Waygood Gallery, Newcastle, UK
*Double Life*, The Waiting Room, Wolverhampton, UK
*Martin*, Top Floor, Atlantis Gallery, London, UK
*Open Ateliers*, Rijksakademie van Beeldende Kunsten, Amsterdam,
The Netherlands
1996 *Childs Play*, D.F.W.T.F.D Gallery, London,UK
*Flag*, Clink Wharf, London, UK
*Life/Live* (with David Medalla, Adam Nakervis and Peter Lewis),
Musée d'Art Moderne de la Ville de Paris, Paris, France
*Yerself is Steam*, 85 Charlotte Road, London, UK
1995 *Lost Property*, The Lost Goods Building, London, UK
1994 *Candyman II*, Building C, London, UK
*Hit and Run 1–4*, Arch 53 and The Ministry of Sound, London,
UK (also 1995, 1996)
Transit at Art Focus, Central Bus Station, Tel Aviv, Israel

## AWARDS, PRIZES AND COMMISSIONS

2001 "Visual Arts Award," London Arts, London, UK
2000 Ford Motor Co & Breakthrough, "Nuture & Desire" Commission
Fondazione Sandretto Re Rebaudengo, "Premio Regione
Piemonte 2000"
1999 University of East London/Richmix Commission Amsterdam
Fonds voor de Kunst "Aanmoedigings Prijs '99"
1998 Rijksakademie van Beeldende Kunsten, "Acquisitions Prize"
Nuffic (The Netherlands Organization for International
Cooperation in Higher Education), The Netherlands
1997 Foundation of Sports and Arts Awards
Campden Charities Scholarship

## BIBLIOGRAPHY


2001 Kent, Sarah, "'Runa Islam,' White Cube." *Time Out*, 2001.
Lewis, Peter. Gymnasium. Bregenz: Kunstverein Bregenz, 2001.
"Runa Islam," *ZOO 10*, (2001): 140.
Valdez, Sarah. "In/SITE/Out:Inquiries into Social Space." *Time Out
New York*, 12–19 April 2001.
Verzotti, Giorgio, and Margaret Shore. "Runa Islam: the White
Cube." *ArtForum 40*, (September 2001): 205.
Wilson, Michael. "Lights, Camera, Action?" *Art Monthly 246*,
(May 2001): 24–5.
2000 Bianchi, Paolo, Fetz, Wolfgang and Sagmeister, Rudolf.
*Kunst in der Stadt 4*. Bregenz: Kunsthaus Bregenz and Bregenzer
Kunstverein, 2000.
Bonami, Francesco. *Guarene Arte 2000*. Guarene D'Alba, Italy:
Fondazione Sandretto Re Rebaudengo per L'Arte, 2000.
Coles, Pippa, Matthew Higgs, and Jacqui Poncelet. *The British Art
Show 5*. London: Hayward Gallery National Touring Exhibitions,
2000.
*<hers> Video as a Female Terrain*. Edited by Stella Rollig. Graz,
Austria: Steirischerherbst, Landesmuseum, Joanneum, 2000.
Kelly, Jo Hill. *Nurture and Desire*. London: Hayward Gallery, 2000.
1999 "Alles great aus den Fugen." *Westdeustche Allgemeine Zeitung*, 1999.
"Alles vergeht-nur die nervosität nicht." *Westfälische Rundschau*,
1999.
Barragan, Paco. "Representando lo invisible." *El Periodico del Arte*,
(1999).
Beech, Dave. "East is East." *Art Monthly*, (1999).
Beech, Dave. "Video After Diderot." *Art Monthly 7*, (1999): 230.
Bruyn, Peter. "Impakt '99 met Jimi Hendrix aan de Draaitafel."
*Utrecht Nieuwsblad*, 1999.
"Dislocation der zweite teil." *Westfälische Rundschau*, 1999.
"Dis-locations." *Flash Art*, (1999).
"Dortmund zieght medien-kunst." *Iserlohner Kreisanzeiger*.

Glibb, Michel. "Deranging the Senses." *Art Monthly*, (1999).
Hagoort, Erik. "Trance en extase bij lieve attacties." *de Volkskrant*
(The Netherlands), 1999.
Hylton, Richard. "Global v Local." *Art Monthly*, (1999).
"Im Rausch der Medien." *Kunst*, (1999).
"Integriete Brechung." *Bodo*, (1999).
"Inszenierte Verischerungen." *Foyer*, (1999).
Jansen, Bert. "Zinnenstrelend." *Het Financieele Dagblad*, 1999.
"Looking East." *Flash Art*, (1999).
Kent, Sarah. "More than Zero." *Time Out* (London) (1999): 45.
Lebovici, Elisabeth. "Big Bangladesh à Londres." *Libération*, (1999).
McEwen, John. "Asses on the Rampage." *The Sunday Telegraph*, 1999.
McTige, Eoghan. "Transgressive Events." *Circa Journal of Art*, (1999).
Moukhatar, Esma. "Prikkels en spiegels." *Skrien*, (1999).
O'Rourke, Imogen. "Back to the Beginning." *Mute*, (1999).
"Schmetterling schlüpft in einem Kunst-Raum." *Ruhrmachrichten*.
Smalleburg, Sandra. "Stimuli." *NRC Handlesblad* (The
Netherlands), 1999.
"Stimuli." *De Witte Raaf*, (1999).
Welling, Dolf. "Artistieke prikkelingen in Witte de With."
*Rotterdams Dagblad*, 1999.
White, Mo. "Never Take Nothing for Granted." *Second Generation*,
(1999).
1998 Bathish, Hani M. "Functional pieces of art on display."
*Khaleej Times*, (1998).
"British Contemporary Art." *Gulf News*, (1999).
Bronwasser, Sacha. "Verbeelding geveed door ontheemding." *de
Volkskrant* (The Netherlands), 1998.
Dunne, Aidan. "Matters of Life and Death." *Irish Times*, (1998).
Mahoney, Elisabeth. "Host." *Contemporary Visual Art*, (1998).
Mahoney, Elisabeth. "A Host of Artists." *The Scotsman*, (1998).
Mulholland, Neil. "Host." *Art Monthly 26*, (1998): 217.
"Sheikh Sultan opens British art exhibition." *The Gulf Today* (1998).
Smallenburg, Sandra. "Open dagen voor jonge kunstenaars." *NRC
Handelsblad*, (The Netherlands), 1998.
"Sultan stresses role of science and technology." *The Gulf Today*,
(1998).
Watson, Gavin. "Giving Birth to Greatness." *Irish Sunday Times*,
(1998).
White, Nicola. "Altogether Now 'Host'." *Glasgow Herald*, (1998).


# TOMOKO TAKE

Born in Osaka, Japan, in 1970
Lives and works in Amsterdam

## EDUCATION/RESIDENCIES

1997 Rijksakademie van Beeldende Kunsten, Amsterdam, The
–98 Netherlands
1994 Kyoto City University of Arts, Kyoto, Japan
–96
1989 Osaka University of Arts, Osaka, Japan
–94

## SOLO EXHIBITIONS

2000 *Chiko & Toko Project*, Stedelijk Museum Bureau Amsterdam,
Amsterdam, The Netherlands
1999 *Dutch Wife/Dutch Life Project*, Window Gallery, Antwerp, Belgium

## GROUP EXHIBITIONS

2002 *Commitment*, Het terrein van de Lightfabriek, Haarlem, The
Netherlands
2001 *Artist Today 2001, Articulate Voice*, Yokohama Civic Art Gallery,
Yokohama, Japan
*KYOTO*AMSTERDAM-New Directions*, Kyoto Art Center, Kyoto, Japan

2000    *Chiko & Toko Project* in *Continental Shift*, Library, Arhen, Germany
        *Continental Shift*, Ludwig Forum Museum, Arhen, Germany
        *For Real*, Stedelijk Museum Bureau Amsterdam, Amsterdam, The
        Netherlands
        *Ideas for Living—Part 2*, De Paviljoens, Almere, The Netherlands
        *Sandburg 2*, Hoorn, The Netherlands
1999    *Chiko & Toko Project* in *10 jaar Fonds BKVB, De Toekomst Die Ons
        Toekomst*, Amsterdam, The Netherlands
        *Chiko & Toko Project* in *Ideas for Living*, Galerie Micheline Szwajcer,
        Antwerp, Belgium
        *Chiko & Toko Project* in *In de ban van de ring*, Nippon Centre and
        Provinciaal Bibliotheek Linburg, Hasselt, Belgium
        *In de ban van de ring*, Stedelijk mode museum and Provinciaal
        centram voor beeldendekunsten—Begijnhof, Hasselt, Belgium
        *Were you there?* Melkfablick, 'sHertogenbosch and Eindhoven, The
        Netherlands (Performance)
        *Werk boven de bank*, Archipel aktuele beeldende kunst, Apeldoon,
        The Netherlands
1998    16th World Wide Video Festival, De Melkweg, Amsterdam, The
        Netherlands
        *Chiko & Toko Project* in *Open Ateliers*, Rijksakademie van Beeldende
        Kunsten, Amsterdam, The Netherlands
        *Lengte, Breedte en Diepte,Twaalf interculturele ontmoetingen*, Geele
        Rijder, Ahnem, The Netherlands
        *Not Strictly Private*, Shed im Eisenwerk, Frauenfeld, Switzerland
        *Open Ateliers*, Rijksakademie van Beeldende Kunsten, Amsterdam,
        The Netherlands
1997    15th World Wide Video Festival, Melkweg, Amsterdam, The
        Netherlands
        *Cloud Chamber*, Ars Electronica Centre, Linz, Austria
        *Open Ateliers*, Rijksakademie van Beeldende Kunsten, Amsterdam,
        The Netherlands
        Performance *Narciss and Echo* with Joan Jonas, Henk Visch, D.J.
        Spooky
1996    Wavering Line, gallery for media art revel on the internet
        (*http://www.wavering.com*)
1995    13th World Wide Video Festival, Den Haag, The Netherlands
1994    12th World Wide Video Festival, Den Haag, The Netherlands
        Selections from 12th World Wide Video Festival, Museo Nacional
        Centro de Arte Reina Sofía Reina, Madrid, Spain

## PRIZES
1998    Uriot prize, Rijksakademie van Beeldende Kunsten, Amsterdam,
        The Netherlands

## COLLECTIONS
        Watari-um museum, Tokyo, Japan; Rijksakademie van Beeldende
        Kunsten, Amsterdam, The Netherlands

## OTHER ACTIVITIES/RECORD RELEASES
1999    *Chiko & Toko Project*, 21e Trans Musicales, Rennes, France
2000    *Chiko & Toko Cooking!* Cooking Theme Song produced.
        Release of remix of *We Love Dancing!*
1999    Release of CD album *All-In*, Emperor Norton Records, USA
        MTV Latino release video clip of *We Love Dancing!* for *Alternative
        Nation*
        Release of 12–inch album *We Love to Rock!*, Emperor Norton
        Records, USA
        *Voulez-vous?* (side B: *We Love Dancing!*) selected one of the best
        CD singles of 1998 by *The New York Times*
1998    Live performance, *Escalator Records All Stars*, Quatro, Osaka &
        Tokyo, Japan
        Release of CD album *Sound Shopping* (special comix edition),
        Basta, The Netherlands
        Release of CD single *We Love Dancing!* and CD album *All-In*, Basta,
        The Netherlands
        Release of 12–inch album *Voulez-vous?* (side B: *We Love Dancing!*),
        Emperor Norton Records in USA

Release of video clip of *We Love Dancing!* for broadcasting.
(Directed by Tomoko Take; produced by Drive-in Productions)

## BIBLIOGRAPHY
2001    A-Prior, Brussels, Belgium: "88", 2001.
        *Articulate Voice*. Yokohama, Japan: Yokohama Civic Art Gallery, 2001.
        BT, (2001).
        *KYOTO*AMSTERDAM-New Directions*. Kyoto, Japan: Kyoto Art
        Center, 2001.
2000    *Amsterdam Stadsblad Centrum*. 1 August 2000.
        BT, (March 2000).
        *Chiko & Toko Cooking*. Amsterdam: Stedelijk Museum Bureau
        Amsterdam, 2000.
        *Continental Shift*. Arhen, Germany: Ludwig Forum Museum, 2000.
        *De Telegraaf*. (Amsterdam) 11 August 2000.
        *de Volkskrant*. (The Netherlands) 26 July 2000.
        *Intercommunication*. (Tokyo, Japan) 32, (spring 2000).
        *NRC Handelsblad*. (Rotterdam) 1 August 2000.
        *For Real*. Amsterdam: Stedelijk Museum Bureau Amsterdam, 2000.
        *Tokion*. (Tokyo, Japan) (January 2000).
        *Where is there?* 'sHertogenbosch and Eindhoven, The Netherlands:
        International Performance Festival, 2000.
1999    *10 jaar Fonds BKVB, De Toekomst Die Ons Toekomst*. Amsterdam,
        The Netherlands, 1999.
        *De Morgen*. (Belgium), February 1999.
        *Metropolis M*. (August 1999).
        *New*. (Amsterdam, The Netherlands) (November 1999).
        *Pulp*. (Belgium) (July 1999).
        *Wonder*. (Antwerp, Belgium) (February 1999).
1998    *16th World Wide Video Festival*. Amsterdam: Melkweg, 1998.
        Bielen Tajblalt. Switzerland, 1998.
        *de Volkskrant*. (The Netherlands), November 1998.
        *De Gele Rijder*, Arnhem, The Netherlands, 1998.
        *Lengte, Breedte en Diepte, Twaalf interculturele ontmoetingen*. (May
        and December 1998).
        *Safe*. (Arhem, The Netherlands) (November 1998).
        *Trouw*. (Amsterdam) (November 1998).
        *Zuriseespiegel*. (Switzerland) (June 1998).

## WEB PAGES
        *http://www.wavering.com/KALEIDO/TTP.HTML*
        *http://www.wwvf.nl/homepage/history/pictures/1998picture_archive.htm*
        *http://www.smba.nl/shows/54/54.htm*


## FIONA TAN

Born in Pekan Baru, Indonesia, in 1966
Lives and works in The Netherlands

## EDUCATION/RESIDENCIES
2001    DAAD scholarship, Berlin, Germany
1996    Rijksakademie van Beeldende Kunsten, Amsterdam, The
–97     Netherlands
1988    Gerrit Rietveld Academie, Amsterdam, The Netherlands
–92

## SOLO EXHIBITIONS
2002    Palais de Beaux Arts, Brussels, Belgium (traveling to Villa Arson,
        Nice, France; Museum De Pont, Tilburg, The Netherlands;
        Hamburger Bahnhof, Hamburg, Germany)
2001    Art Unlimited, Art 32 Basel, Switzerland
        *Fiona Tan, Rain*, Elisabeth Kaufmann, Zürich, Switzerland
        *Fiona Tan, Recent Works*, Galerie Michel Rein, Paris, France
        *Matrix 144*, Wadsworth Atheneum Museum of Art, Hartford, CT,
        USA

*May You Live in Interesting Times*, Erfrischungsraum, Die Galerie der Hochschule Für Gestaltung und Kunst Luzern, Luzern, Switzerland
Wako Works of Art, Japan

2000  *Carwreck Cinema*, Aussendienst Hamburg, Germany
Galleria Massimo de Carlo, Milan, Italy
*Lift*, Galerie Paul Andriesse, Amsterdam, The Netherlands
*Scenario*, Kunstverein Hamburg, Germany

1999  *Cradle*, Galerie Paul Andriesse, Amsterdam, The Netherlands
*Roll I & II*, Museum De Pont, Tilburg, The Netherlands
*Smoke Screen*, De Balie, Amsterdam, The Netherlands
*Solo*, De Begane Grond, Utrecht, The Netherlands

1998  *J.C. Van Lanschot Prijs*, S.M.A.K., Ghent, Belgium
*Linneaus' Flower Clock*, Stedelijk Museum Het Domein, Sittard, The Netherlands

1997  *Open Ateliers*, Rijksakademie van Beeldende Kunst, Amsterdam, The Netherlands

1996  *Open Ateliers*, Rijksakademie van Beeldende Kunst, Amsterdam, The Netherlands

1995  *Inside Out*, Montevideo, Galerie René Coelho, Amsterdam, The Netherlands

## GROUP EXHIBITIONS/SCREENINGS/PROJECTS

2002  *Selfexposure*, Rijksuniversiteit Groningen, The Netherlands
*Thin Skin*, AXA Gallery, New York, NY, USA
*tele-journeys*, MIT List Visual Arts Center, Cambridge, MA, USA

2001  2. Berlin Biennale, Berlin, Germany
*Enduring Love*, Klemens Gasser & Tanja Grunert, Inc., New York, NY
*Endtroducing*, Villa Arson, Nice, France
*Futureland*, Städtisches Museum Abteiberg, Mönchengladbach, Germany, and Museum Bommel van Dam, Venlo, The Netherlands
*Mobile Walls*, Museum Boijmans Van Beuningen, Rotterdam, The Netherlands
*My Generation: 24 Hours of Video Art*, Atlantis Gallery, London, UK
*Plateau of Mankind*, 49th Venice Biennale, Venice, Italy
*Recente aanwinsten*, Stedelijk Museum Bureau Amsterdam, Amsterdam, The Netherlands
*Sculpture Contemporaine*, Institut d'art contemporain, Lyon, France
Yokohama 2001 International Triennial of Contemporary Art, Yokohama, Japan

2000  *Cinema Without Walls*, Museum Boijmans van Beuningen, Rotterdam, The Netherlands
*Everything Needs Time*, St. Michael's Church, Honiton; Thelma Hulbert Gallery, Honiton; Spacex Gallery; Exeter, UK
*Et l'art se met au monde*, Institute d'art contemporain, Villeurbanne, France
*Etat des lieux #2*, Centre d'art Contemporain, Fribourg, Switzerland
Finsternis/Finsterre, Palazzo delle Pappesse, Pisa, Italy
<hers> Video as a Female Terrain, Steirischerherbst, Landesmuseum Joanneum Graz, Austria
*Kingdom of Shadows*, 2000, (documentary) screened in national cinemas and at the IDFA in Amsterdam
*Shanghai Spirit*, Shanghai Biennale 2000, Shanghai Art Museum, Shanghai, China
*Still/Moving*, Museum of Modern Art Kyoto, Kyoto, Japan

1999  *8e Biennale de l'Image en Mouvement*, Centre pour l'Image Contemporaine, Geneve, Switzerland
*Cities on the Move*: Hayward Gallery, London, UK; Louisiana Museum, Humlebæk, Denmark; Kiasma Museum of Contemporary Art, Helsinki, Finland
*Go Away*, Royal College of Art, London, UK
*International Biennale of Photography*, Centro de la Imagen, Mexico City, Mexico
*Life Cycles*, Galerie fur Zeitgenossische Kunst, Leipzig, Germany
*The Power of Beauty*, Gemeentemuseum Helmond, The Netherlands
*The Second*, Ludwig Museum, Budapest, Hungary

*Stimuli*, Witte de With, Rotterdam, The Netherlands
*Zug (luft)*, Museum Kurhaus Kleve, Germany

1998  *+8 +7 +3 +1 −1 −5*, Glass Box, Paris; I.A.I., Moscow, Russia
*Biennale de l'Image Paris '98*, E.N.S.B.A, Paris, France
*Cities on the Move*, PS1 Contemporary Art, New York, NY, USA; CAPC Musée d'art contemporain de Bordeaux, France
*Déplacements*, Galerie Anton Weller, Paris, France
*Entrè-fiction*, Centre d'Art Contemporaine Rueil-Malmaison, France
*Power Up*, Gemeentemuseum Arnhem, The Netherlands
*Rineke Dijkstra, Tracey Moffatt, Fiona Tan*, S.M.A.K., Ghent, Belgium
*Scope*, Artists Space, New York, NY, USA
*The Second-Time Based Art from the Netherlands*, Fine Arts Museum, Taipei, Taiwan; ICC, Tokyo, Japan
*Traces of Science in Art*, Het Trippenhuis, Amsterdam, The Netherlands
*Unlimited.nl−2*, De Appel, Amsterdam, The Netherlands
16th World Wide Video Festival, Melkweg, and Stedelijk Museum Bureau Amsterdam, Amsterdam, The Netherlands

1997  *2nd Johannesburg Biennale*, Johannesburg, South Africa
*Cities on the Move*, Wiener Secession, Vienna, Austria
*Hong Kong-Parfumed Harbour*, De Appel, Amsterdam, Tne Netherlands
*The Second-Time Based Art from the Netherlands*, Stedelijk Museum Bureau *Amsterdam*, Amsterdam, The Netherlands; Museo Del Chopo, Mexico

1996  *hARTware projekte−Dutch Media Art in the '90s*, Künstlerhaus, Dortmund, Germany

1995  *Arslab−I Sensi del Virtuale*, Palazzo della Belli Arti, Turin, Italy
*Beyond the Bridge*, Nederlands Filmmuseum, Amsterdam, The Netherlands

1994  Stedelijk Museum Bureau Amsterdam, Amsterdam, The Netherlands

## PRIZES

1998  J.C. Van Lanschot Prize for Sculpture, Belgium/The Netherlands
1997  Best National Debut Film, Nederlands Filmfestival, The Netherlands
1995  *Arslab i Sensi del Virtuale*, Turin, Italy

## BIBLIOGRAPHY

2001  Ardenne, P. "Fiona Tan." *Art Press* 269, (2001): 82.
Bem, M. "Toekomst zoals de kunstenaar die voelt." *de Volkskrant* (The Netherlands), 27 October 2001, 7.
Berg, R. "Die Kunst-Kommissarin." *Zitty* 9, (April 2001): Jrg.24.
Bers, M. "Berlin Biennale: Affect, Not Effect." *Tema Celeste* 86, (2001): 74–79.
Breerette, G. "Le journal intime de Fiona Tan, vidéasté." *Le Monde*, 15–16 April 2001, 18.
Durez, A. "Fiona Tan, Usage de la disparition." *Centre national de la photographie, le journal* 15, (2001): 11.
Erno, A. "Fiona Tan, du temps au temps." *l'Humanité hebdo*, 12–13 May 2001.
Flether, Annie. "Fiona Tan: a conversation between Fiona Tan and Annie Flether." *2. Berlin Biennale*. Edited by Saskia Bos, with contributions by Annie Fletcher, Charles Esche, Daniel Birnbaum, Nicolas Bourriaud, et al. Cologne: Oktagon, 2001, 250–253.
Gioni, M. "Speaking in Tongues, Views from a Distance." *Flash Art* 34, (November-December 2001): 74–77.
McNally, O. "Filmmaker's Atheneum Show Mixes Old, New." *The Hartford Courant*, 17 May 2001.
Müller, S. "Energie geben statt provozieren." *ART das kunst-magazin* 4, (April 2001): 78–83.
Psibiliskis, L. "Gesichter in der Optik einer Fixkamera." *Kunst-Bulletin*, (October 2001): 18–21.
Roelandt, E. "Japan ontdekt impact hedendaagse kunst." *Financieel Economische Tijd*, 17 November 2001.
Rosoff, P. "If I Fell to Earth Full Grown." *The Hartford Advocate*, 31 May 2001, 19.

Ruthe, I. "Von der Verlorenheit zwischen den Welten." *Berliner Zeitung*, 26–27 May 2001.

Tan, Fiona. *Marebito*. (artist's book, limited edition of 500, signed and numbered by the artist, 2001).

Tilroe, A. "Dansen met de Mexicanse superman." *NRC Handelsblad* (The Netherlands) (Cultureel Supplement), 27 April 2001.

Wit, Katrin. "Fiona Tan." *Berliner Tageszeitung*, 13 April 2001.

2000   Asthoff, J. "Loop des Lebens." *Szene Hamburg*, (April 2000).

Groß, O. "Wie die Wilden." *Hamburger Rundschau*, 27 March 2000.

IvdV. "Het wonder van het bewegende beeld." *VPRO-gids*, 57.

Jahn, W. "Auf der Suche nach Authentizität." *Hamburger Abendblatt*, 17 April 2000.

Koll, G. "Das Leben als Fremdkörper." *Kieler Nachrichten*, 19 April 2000.

Monshouwer S. "Een kinderdroom." *Kunstbeeld 9*, (September 2000): 17.

Pontzen, R. "De 'loop' maakt de beweging statisch." *Kunstblad* (The Netherlands) 3, (December 2000): 21–23.

Prins W. "Fiona Tan: Scenario." *Kunstblad* (The Netherlands) 3, (December 2000).

Stecker, R. "Fiona Tan im Kunstverein." *Kunst-Bulletin*, (June 2000).

"Suggestive Szenen." *Hamburger Abendblatt*, 6 March 2000.

Tan, Fiona. *Scenario*. Amsterdam: Vandenberg & Wallroth, 2000.

Van Elsberg, J. "Fiona Tan: duizendpoot met vele gezichten." *Skrien* jrg 32, 9, (2000): 66.

Wijnja, N. "Bubbelbad." *Het Parool* (Amsterdam, The Netherlands), 8 September 2000, 9.

1999   Dorment, R. "It's not art-it's agitprop." *The Daily Telegraph*, 28 April 1999.

Hagoort, E. "Trance en extase bij lieve attracties." *de Volkskrant* (The Netherlands), 4 December 1999, 8.

Herst, D. "Fiona Tan." *Creative Camera 360*, (October–November 1999).

Moukhtar, E. "Smoke Screen; Tussen beeld en blik." *Skrien 236*, (1999): 60–61.

Steevens, B. "Het absolute bestaat niet." *Metropolis M 1*, (1999).

Süto, W. "Mijn tong is niet mijn beste vriend." *de Volkskrant* (The Netherlands), 16 April 1999.

Tan, Fiona. "Rookgordijn." *Filmkrant 203*, (September 1999).

Tan, Fiona. "Tegenbeeld." *Metropolis M 4*, (1999).

1998   Didier, M. "De tijd vangen." *De Groene Amsterdammer*, 16 September 1998.

Groot, P. "Nederland speciaal." *Metropolis M*, (March 1998).

Hoekendijk, C. "Fiona Tan, Linneaus' Flower Clock." *World Wide Video Festival*. Amsterdam: World Wide Video Festival, 1998.

Lamoree, J. "Denken doet wonderen." *Het Parool* (Amsterdam, The Netherlands), 25 July 1998, 14.

Roelandt, E. "Rokende baby's en 'ravende' jongeren." *De Morgen*, 30 March 1998.

Smallenburg, S. "Fiona Tan vat herinneringen in video." *NRC Handelsblad* (The Netherlands), 16 September 1998.

Sierksma, P. "Wim Beeren en het trage geluid van opspattend water." *Trouw*, 6 August 1998.

Tan, Fiona. "Brief aan Chantal Akkerman." *Skrien*, (30 year jubilee number 1998).

Tan, Fiona. *Open Heart* (a correspondance between Fiona Tan and writer Robert Vernooy). Amsterdam: De Balie, 1998.

Tan, Fiona. "Smoke Screen." *Lover tijdschrift 3*.

Ter Borg, L. *Fiona Tan, Linnneaus' Flower Clock*. Amsterdam: Het Trippenhuis KNAW, 1998.

Westen, M. "Fiona Tan" in *Power Up*. Arnhem: Museum voor Moderne Kunst, 1998.

1997   Hal, M. van. "Time based art." *Wave*, (January 1997).

Lammers, F. "Éen huwlijk van culturen." *Trouw*, 23 July 1997.

Lamoree, J. "De nieuwe media verslaan de oude." *Het Parool* (Amsterdam, The Netherlands), 27 November 1997.

Linssen, D. "Interessante tijden." *NRC Handelsblad* (The Netherlands), 25 July 1997.

Schwartz, I. "Time Strechter laat lijf golven." *de Volkskrant* (The Netherlands), 9 April 1997.

Tan, Fiona. *Collecting Presents* (*Hong Kong*) Amsterdam: RABK. 1997.

Tan, Fiona. "Dagboeknotities van jonge cineasten-Het verzamelen van cadeautjes." *Skrien 213*, (April–May 1997).

Tan, Fiona. *Fragments towards a selfportrait of a city I & II*. (*Hong Kong*). Amsterdam: RABK, 1997.

1996   Beerekamp, H. "De Brug." *NRC Handelsblad* (The Netherlands), 6 December 1996.

"Medienkunst aus die Niederlanden." *Kunst Kurier*, (March 1996).

Vries, M. de. "De dans van wellustig levend plasma. *Het Parool* (Amsterdam, The Netherlands), 13 December 1996.

1995   Lamoree, J. "Landje pik in het Siberie van Amsterdam." *Het Parool* (Amsterdam, The Netherlands), 8.

"Plakjes mens–Atlas of the Interior van Fiona Tan." *BLVD*, (November 1995).

Smallenburg S. "Beyond the Bridge." *HTV de Ijsberg* (December 1995).

Visser, N. van "Nadenken over plakjes moordenaar." *Het Parool* (Amsterdam, The Netherlands), 17 March 1995.

**CARLOS AMORALES**
*Amorales Interim;  Arena Dos de Mayo; Ray Rosas,* 1997
3 VHS videotapes (*Amorales Interim,* 4 min. 13 sec.; *Arena Dos de Mayo,* 13 min. 59 sec.; *Ray Rosas,* 50 min. 57 sec.); 3 monitors
Collection MGB, Migros Museum für Gegenwartskunst, Zurich

**CARLOS AMORALES**
*Amorales vs. Amorales,* 1990–2001
4 DVD projections (*El Olympico,* 16 minutes, 22 seconds; *Amorales,* 27 min., 30 sec.; *El Bucanero,* 22 min., 50 sec.; *My Way,* 15 min., 58 sec.); 4 monitors
Collection MGB, Migros Museum für Gegenwartskunst, Zurich

**CARLOS AMORALES**
*Solitario* (Solitary), 1998
VHS videotape, 14 min., 12 sec.; monitor
Collection Walker Art Center, Minneapolis
T.B. Walker Acquisition Fund, 1999

**CARLOS AMORALES**
*Super Barrio; Interim Performance; Table Dance,* 1997
VHS videotapes on monitors, each approximately 7 min.
Courtesy of the artist

**MARK BAIN**
*Sniffer,* 2002
Steel, aluminum, electronic components, 35" long x 6" diameter
Courtesy of the artist

**YAEL BARTANA**
*Trembling Time,* 2001
DVD projection, 6 min., 10 sec.
Courtesy of the artist

**YAEL BARTANA**
*Profile,* 2000
DVD, 2 min, 49 sec.; monitor
Courtesy of the artist

**MICHAEL BLUM**
*Wandering Marxwards,* 1999
VHS videotape, 19 min., 22 sec.; monitor
Courtesy of the artist

**NABILA IRSHAID**
*Travel Agency,* 2001
VHS videotape, 7 min., 30 sec.; monitor
Courtesy of the artist

**RUNA ISLAM**
*Tuin,* 1998
2 DVD projections, 2 CDs, 16 mm film, approximately 6 min.
Courtesy of Jay Jopling/White Cube, London

**SEBASTIAN DIAZ MORALES**
*15,000,000 Parachutes,* 2001
DVD projection, 25 min.
Courtesy of the artist

**TOMOKO TAKE**
*Dutch Wife/Dutch Life,* 1996–2001
DVD projection, 94 min.
Courtesy of the artist

**FIONA TAN**
*May You Live in Interesting Times,* 1997
DVD projection, 59 min., 8 sec.
Courtesy Galerie Paul Andriesse, Amsterdam

**FIONA TAN**
*Rain,* 2001
2 DVDs, 2 video monitors, metal brackets, and shelves
Courtesy Galerie Paul Andriesse, Amsterdam

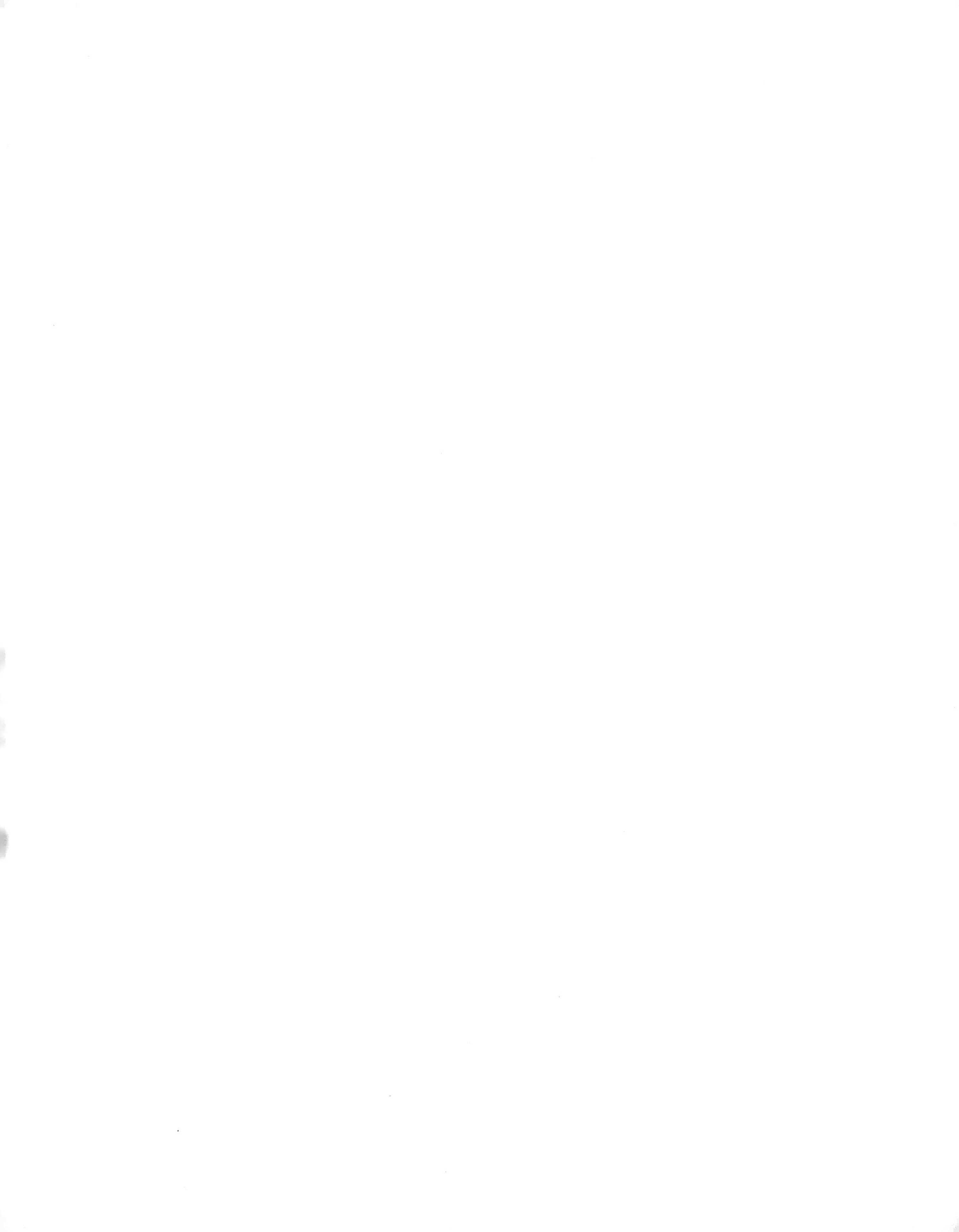

PHOTO CREDITS
Unless otherwise noted, all photos are courtesy of the artist.
p.14: Photo courtesy of Migros Museum für Gegenwartskunst, Zurich.
p.15: Photo courtesy of Walker Art Center, Minneapolis, MN.
pp.24/25: Photos courtesy of Jay Jopling (London).
pp.30/31: Photos courtesy of Galerie Paul Andriesse, Amsterdam.